A JOURNEY INTO OPIOID HELL AND BACK

My Recovery from Prescription Narcotics

Lizzy Wisniewski

10-10-10 Publishing

A JOURNEY INTO OPIOID HELL AND BACK:
My Recovery from Prescription Narcotics

Copyright © 2021 Lizzy Wisniewski

ISBN: 978-1-77277-410-8

The suggestions in this book for personal healing and recovery are not meant to substitute for the advice of a licensed health professional such as a medical doctor or psychiatrist. It is essential to consult such a professional in the case of any physical or mental symptoms. The publisher and author expressly disclaim any liability for injuries resulting from use by readers of the methods contained herein.

I have tried to recreate events, locales and conversations from my memories of them. In order to maintain their anonymity, I have changed the names of individuals and places, I may have changed some identifying characteristics and details such as physical properties, occupations and places of residence. Any resemblance to a living person is purely by chance.

Publisher
10-10-10 Publishing
Markham, ON Canada

Printed in Canada and the United States of America

Table of Contents

*This book is dedicated in loving memory to my parents,
Cecilia and Ziggy Wisniewski, who taught me
strong work ethics, compassion, kindness,
and a strong love of family and friends.*

*This book is dedicated in loving memory to my brother,
Ronnie, who I miss every day.*

*This book is dedicated in loving memory to Ed Francisco,
a dear friend who helped me greatly
while I was in Ottawa.*

*This book is also dedicated to my sister, Eley,
who is my best friend in the entire universe, and my strongest
advocate. Without her help, guidance, patience, and care,
I know that I would not have survived
this addiction and withdrawal.
She continues to lift me up, keep me strong,
and make me laugh.*

Acknowledgements

First, I want to thank God for keeping me alive. There were many days and nights when I prayed to You, with tears running down my cheeks, that I wouldn't die from all of these drugs. I felt so lost and scared, but as promised, You led me out of the vast darkness into Your light. Thank you for hearing my prayers, my pleas, and my supplications, and for answering them as only You can. You surrounded me with my loving family and friends who helped me to heal, and who led me to those whose medical knowledge and abilities I so desperately needed. To get through this, You gave me strength and courage that I never knew I had, and for that, I thank You.

Second, to my dear sister, Eley; I know that I would not be alive today without your constant love and care. You saw how these drugs ravaged my body and mind, but you stood beside me each step of the way. Your sheer determination in finding someone who could help me was unstoppable. Your positivity helped me take one step forward, again and again, even when I had taken two steps back. You were my legal caregiver for three and a half years while I withdrew from all of these drugs, and I know it wasn't easy to live through or watch. But you never gave up on me. You were and are my best friend and advocate. I want to thank you from the bottom of my heart for searching until you finally found a doctor who could help us: Dr. Eileen Groves. Thank you for sticking with me through everything. You are an angel here on earth (although I'm not sure where you hide your wings), and I love you with all my "serca" (heart in Polish).

To my brother, Ziggy, thanks for always being my protector. You are the best "driving instructor," whether it was teaching me how to drive a tractor, a truck, or a car. I am so blessed to have such a kind, supportive, and loving "big" brother.

To my brother, Ronnie, who is now with God, you couldn't understand why I stayed in Ottawa so long when I was so sick. But I thought I would get better and go back to work. I guess you just wanted me closer so that you could tease me, like you always did! I miss you and love you, Uggy.

To my brother, Eddie, thanks for making me laugh. I know that you have been an auctioneer for years, but you have to remember that when someone is on a lot of drugs, you need to speak slower!!! You always have a story to tell, and the laughter made me feel better.

To my sister-in-law, Darlene, you started dating Ziggy when I was 6 years old, so I feel like you've always been part of the family. I am so grateful for our friendship and for your sense of direction, because Ziggy would be lost, A LOT. Thank you for all of your support and understanding, especially during my sickness. Thanks to you and Ziggy, I have three nephews—Jamie, Joe, and Mike—of whom I am so proud.

To my sister-in-law, Marti, you are an exceptionally caring and supportive person. I always told Ronnie that the best thing he did was marry you! You are a dear friend, and I treasure our friendship. Thanks to you and Ronnie, I have 2 nephews, Trevor and David, of whom I am so proud.

To my best friends, Michelle (aka Chelka) and John, and my godchildren, Amber and PJ Connell. You, too, were witnesses to some of my darkest moments. Thank you for convincing me to move back "home," where you could be right around the corner when I needed you. Thanks for all the rides to my many doctor's appointments and the odd emergency room visit. You knew the car ride would be awful, with every bump causing me to scream out in pain, but you took me anyway. I'm so glad that you now like going for car rides with me! Chelka, you were always there to listen when I called you crying because I felt like I was just not getting any better. You would always reply, "But

Lizzy, look how far you've come!" Thanks for your encouragement; it was and is such a great help.

To my relatives who I lovingly call "The Wigilia (Christmas Eve) Group"—Tom and Laraine Belbeck, Carol and Rick Daley, Henry Krukowski, Natasha Mohammed-Wisniewski, Jelena Hossack, the Regos (Dennis, Michelle, Sophia and Ben), the Belbecks (Jeff, Ange, Holly and Owen), Susan Daley, Sharon Daley, and the Potomas (Rick, Jenn and Emma)—what an incredible group of people you are. I want to thank you for all of your support and love. You are not only my family but my dear friends. When I was so ill that I had to lie down after just arriving at your homes for a meal, you still kept inviting me back. When I would have to leave early because I was feeling so unwell, you still called me later to see how I was. You have been so understanding and kind to me, even when I was slurring my words and probably didn't make sense. You never gave up hope that I would get better. Thank you for keeping me involved in our family gatherings, which mean the world to me.

To Leszek and Basia Wiszniewski, Ania Malec, Joanna and Dino De Faveri, and Stefan and Olenka Blaszyk, thank you for your love and support throughout my life. I am so lucky to have such loving relatives.

To my best friends, Linda Kassay, Donna Spera, and Teresa Jazbec, I am so very blessed that I met you in my teens. We have really been through everything in each other's lives, and our bond is unbreakable. You have each played such an important role in my life that words are inadequate in describing how much you mean to me. We've shared so many fabulous, fun times with all of our crazy antics. I cherish our friendships and am blessed to have your love and support. Thanks to Boris Jazbec for your support as well.

To Rick Stys, you are my best "guy" friend, and our friendship of over 40 years is one that I treasure. You were always so concerned about my health when you would call to chat. Thank you to you and your wife, Lisa, and your fabulous kids, Lukas and

Nicholas, for your continued support and love.

To my dearest friends in Ottawa and Newfoundland—Roxanne Galway, Sharon Hartin, David Strowbridge, Kim Hwang, Kevin Hill, Theresa O'Connor, and Diane Byrne—you all cheat at cards! Okay, but seriously, how can I ever thank you for all you did? You made living in Ottawa and Orleans fun, and you saw me in my prime, before all this craziness hit. Then you all were concerned and confused as you saw my continued decline into the world of addiction. Thanks for all the phone calls and visits to make sure I was okay. I know you called Eley with updates because you were so worried about me living on my own. Your friendship means the world to me, and I am lucky to call you my friends.

To Mary Jane and Randy Pocrnick, thanks for your friendship and support. From sharing our dreams in university to our lives today, I am so blessed to have you in my life!

To my dear friend, Remy Francisco, and her late husband, Ed Francisco, your love and kindness made my days easier. I can't even begin to count how many times you drove me to doctor's appointments, did my groceries, did my errands, and called to check on me. When you drove me to the emergency department for my first "drug reaction," I remember us praying The Lord's Prayer together, because you thought I was having a stroke! We had a lot of laughs too, especially when I would get "giggly." Thank you so much for all you did to help me, and for being my friend.

To Dr. Kiara, my craniosacral specialist and dear, dear friend: It's been quite the journey, hasn't it, Kiara? From our initial meeting, when I couldn't stay awake, to now, I knew God led us to you, with your amazing healing capabilities and knowledge. You are an incredibly gifted, brilliant physician. Your ability to think outside of the box in using modalities (micro current, laser therapy, and craniosacral therapy) to help treat me, saved my life. You were, and still are, an integral part of my healing, and I am proud to call you a dear friend. Thank you from the bottom of my heart!

To Donna Maljar, we have been friends for decades, and you are also the best hairstylist in the world! You saw me at my worst, and when I came in for a haircut, you had a frozen bag of peas ready so that I could put it on my back to ease my pain. Thanks to you and your husband, Jerry Maljar, for your continued support and love.

To Karen Blundon and Jim Blundon, my ex-next-door neighbours in Orleans, thank you for always checking in on me. Your kindness and friendship are truly gifts. Karen, thank you for the delicious, homemade meals you would deliver to me when you knew I was in no shape to cook anything for myself. Those meals nourished me and my soul.

To my friend, Ancaster school mate, and family doctor in Ottawa, Dr. Lisa, thank you for always having my back. You searched for years for answers in my case, and believed that I had real pain when others did not. Thank you for the hours you spent helping me and guiding me.

To Dr. Julie my family doctor, I know that my long and powerful list of medications scared you the first time you saw it. I mean, who can WALK INTO a doctor's office while taking that many narcotics? But I did, and together, we tackled the withdrawal strategically. Thank you for continuing to help me when I hit those bumps in the road with my back pain, and for your encouragement. I really appreciate all your help.

To my personal book architect, Naval Kumar, thanks for guiding me and keeping me on track to write and publish this book. I truly appreciate your knowledge and expertise.

To all of my friends from the PCAY (Polish Canadian Alliance of Youth), thanks for the kindness, friendship, and loads of fun we've had over the years. I am so blessed to have such fun-loving friends with whom I can share my life. I am so grateful that there were no videos back then! Thanks for sharing my heritage and my life.

To Trisha and Bill Smith, you are both such caring friends. We met when I was at my sickest, and you were always there to offer help and assistance. You are both incredibly kind, and I really love being able to call you my friends.

Foreword

I first met Lizzy Wisniewski when she attended my Speaker and Communication Workshop. I was amazed when she introduced herself as having conquered a narcotic addiction, and shocked to learn that all of the narcotics had been prescribed by a doctor!

A Journey into Opioid Hell and Back is unique, because it will challenge your perception of an "addict." Contrary to the common stereotype of a homeless person living under a bridge hooked on drugs, Lizzy was a fully functioning, contributing member of society. She had a full-time job, did volunteer work, had many friends and enjoyed a busy social life. However, after several years suffering from a back injury without proper pain control, she was referred to a doctor for pain management. Lizzy was prescribed massive amounts of narcotics by that pain specialist, and was reduced to a shell of her former self. She was almost immobile, was sleeping 22 hours a day and barely surviving. Her body was completely addicted to these narcotics and needed them just to "function."

Lizzy will pull you into her debilitating world of addiction, and the painful, horrific withdrawal process. The fact that Lizzy "got clean" without going to a treatment center or using methadone is astonishing. Through her sheer will and determination to survive, she overcame her addiction. Her successful recovery is exemplary, and shows what you can accomplish when you really want something.

This book highlights the courage, strength and hope that can be found within you, even under the most trying of circumstances.

I highly recommend this book!

Raymond Aaron
New York Times Bestselling Author

Introduction

Picture this scenario: You are doing some gardening on a bright, sunny day in your front yard. While digging out a small, dead cedar bush, you go to pull it out, and you feel something go "snap" in your back. The pain is immediate and intense. So, you walk carefully back inside your house, gingerly sit on your sofa, and stay there. The next day, since the pain is still unbearable, even with the ibuprofen you've been taking, you go to your doctor's. The doctor determines that you need a stronger pain pill, so they give you a prescription for one. You fill the prescription, take the pills as prescribed, and are back to work in a couple of weeks, just like your doctor predicted. It's pretty common, isn't it?

Now let's fast forward five years. You are washing dishes at your kitchen sick when you gather some food scraps off a plate. As you bend down to put these in the garbage, your back goes into horrific spasms and you drop to the floor in pain. The pain is unlike anything you've experienced before. You spend the rest of the day immobile in complete agony, even after taking an ibuprofen every 6 hours. The next day, with the help of a friend, you go back to your doctor's like you did years before. You receive a prescription for the latest and greatest new pain pill, get the pills from the pharmacy, and start taking them as directed. You figure you'll be back to work in a couple of weeks, just like before.

But what if the pain never goes away? **For years?** You see doctor after doctor until you find a pain specialist, who is called in to help you "manage" your pain. *Finally*, you think, *someone who can make me feel better!* But what if that doctor just keeps increasing the dosage of this new pill? And the pain keeps increasing? And now this powerful narcotic has made you an "addict" because your body can't function without it?

Some of you may be thinking, *well, that could NEVER happen to me.* Oh really? Think again.

<u>You</u> are only one narcotic prescription away from becoming an addict. I should know, because that's exactly what happened to me.

Even up to this day, I have never bought, nor consumed, an illegal drug—ever, not even marijuana. I have never injected myself with any drugs, never snorted any drugs, nor overconsumed prescription medication.

But I was prescribed the "latest and greatest new pain pill," OxyContin (oxycodone). Even though you probably can't name 10 other prescription drugs on the market today, I bet you've heard about OxyContin. It's the powerfully addictive narcotic at the center of the national and international opioid crisis. So many people are overdosing and dying from taking OxyContin that hospitals are now required to track these horrific statistics weekly. And unfortunately, the numbers continue to rise at an alarming rate.

This one drug changed the entire trajectory of my life, and ruined **YEARS** of my life. No one told me it would take years to get off of it. How can your doctor possibly prepare you for the hell that is withdrawal, when they've only read about the symptoms in a book? This drug not only wreaked havoc on my body and life, but it also caused those I love most to suffer with me as well, as they watched what I had to go through. And I'm one of the lucky ones—I survived.

I've gained immeasurable experience and insight during this enormous challenge. There were many dark times when I wasn't sure I would win this battle, but for me, there was no other choice. I had to keep fighting to get my health and life back.

As you read this book, my goal is that you can be inspired by my journey and be filled with hope to tackle your biggest challenge.

Chapter 1

How on Earth Did I End Up Here?

It's August 21, 2008. I am sitting in Dr. Eileen Groves' office in Burlington, Ontario, with Eley, my sister, waiting to meet this doctor who I've been told can work miracles. And boy, I sure could use one. I'm the sickest I've ever been.

I have been off work since February 5, 2005—over 3½ years—because of excruciating lower back pain. I have seen 53 doctors so far and am not any closer to finding a diagnosis. At this point in my life, **I am barely able to stay awake 2 hours total in a 24-hour DAY!!!** I am now taking 13 different medications, all prescribed, including some very potent narcotics, which have turned me into a walking zombie. I am so drugged that I can't even speak without slurring my words. I can't find the right words. I can't walk straight. I can't concentrate. I can't focus. I can't retain information. I can't remember. I can't find any relief from this constant pain. I can't stay awake. And all I want to do is sleep. I am so tired and sore.

Getting Ready

I need Eley's help just to get ready for the appointment. You just don't understand how much energy it takes to do simple tasks like taking a shower, when you are as sick as I am. Eley won't let me shower alone … oh, wait, that came out wrong …

Eley won't let me shower without her standing in the bathroom supervising me (that's better) in case I fall. When she asks me if I think I can wash my own hair in the shower, I say, "I'll try." I put some shampoo in my right hand and brace myself against the shower wall with the other. So far so good. Then I put my right hand on my head and start rubbing in the shampoo. That's when the room starts spinning. I stop rubbing my head, but the spinning doesn't stop. I feel like I'm on one of those Tilt-a-Whirl rides at the fair. I'm trying to steady myself by grabbing onto the shower curtain, with my shampoo-covered right hand slipping down the curtain while my left hand is grasping for something to hold on the slippery tile. That's when I feel Eley's hands grab me, and the room finally stops. She says, "Let me help you."

With her help, I sit on the side of the tub, and she finishes washing my hair. She braces my body while securing my arm, and helps me stand up under the shower head to wash off the shampoo. I manage to wash the front of my torso but then Eley takes over. If I try to wash my back, that twisting motion of reaching my arm behind me is enough to make my back spasm. I am clenching my teeth because every touch on my back is like an electric shock. I am trying to stifle my pain while the tears run down my face. Luckily, Eley can't see my tears when I'm in the shower.

"Okay, can you lift your right leg out of the tub?" I am so tired from all of this that my leg feels like it weighs 600 lbs. I try my best, but I need Eley's strength to get my leg out of the tub. "Okay, just get your balance while I dry you off." I stand as well as I can while Eley works quickly. "Okay, let's have the other leg." I grab the door that is near the tub, for balance, and try to swing my left leg out of the tub. It drags along the bottom of the tub because I can't seem to lift it. I know it's attached to me, but it's not paying attention to what I want it to do. Again, Eley reaches around my leg and guides it out of the tub. Then she dries off my leg and tells me, "Lift up your right foot so that I can dry the bottom." I try to lift it as high as I can, but I don't know if it's enough. Eley quickly dries it off and then we repeat the process for my other foot. All of this is so exhausting that I just want to go back to bed.

Eley blow dries my short hair for me, which is a luxury because, normally, I would just let it dry naturally. I mean, why waste my effort, as I don't have any to spare at the moment.

Window of Opportunity

You see, we've actually done all of this the night before, because:

taking a shower, AND
getting dressed, AND
going somewhere

are too many tasks for this sick girl to accomplish in a 24-hour period. I know, most people do it without even batting an eye, but for someone who is in chronic pain and horribly drugged, that list is way too long to accomplish in a day. So, we've had to split those tasks between two days; that way, I am hoping to still have enough energy to get to the doctor's. When you are only awake for 2 hours per day, it's a challenge to fit the most important things within that time frame.

The next morning, I am like a little kid who needs help getting dressed. I can't do up my own bra because it does up in the back. I just can't reach back there right now. Then I have to balance on Eley so that she can help me put on my underwear and pants. Lifting one foot and then the other takes a lot of balance even when I am sitting down. Eley then helps me get my t-shirt on quickly so that my arms aren't over my head for too long. That type of movement could cause awful back spasms, which I avoid at all costs. Finally, I'm dressed.

Although I still have my license, I don't drive anymore … for everyone's safety! While most people enjoy going for a drive, for me, at this point, it is hell on earth … and Eley knows this firsthand. Even though she isn't looking forward to the 45-minute drive each way any more than I am, what other options do we have?

I know what you are probably thinking: *C'mon, how hard is it to hop in a car and drive for 45 minutes?* Well, first things first, I can't hop … into or out of anything. I can barely walk by myself, so Eley leads me to the front door and I sit down on a solid chair with a back on it. Eley tells me to wait until she gets the car out of the garage, and then she'll come back for me. Now, she isn't just backing the car out of the garage onto the driveway. She is backing it out of our driveway, onto the road, and parking it in front of our house. You see, that little bump that everyone has where your driveway meets the street, for me, is like dropping to the earth's core, which sends spasms up my back.

Eley gets out of the car to help me into it. My driveway, which is only slightly longer than 2 car lengths, feels like I am crossing a football field. Plus, it is uneven and slopes to the road, which causes extra pressure on my back. The car door is open, so Eley helps me turn myself around in order to "back into" the car, bum first. I know this is going to hurt because not only is this a level change (standing to sitting), but Eley has bucket seats, which are an uneven surface. I brace myself and sit down on the edge of the seat. Oh, my God, that really hurt, but I know I'm not done yet. I have to reposition myself to sit in the seat correctly. The seat is dipped in the middle by design, which means my pelvis is shifting while moving into position. And it is causing pain from my pelvis to my neck. It feels like a steel rod is piercing me up both sides of my spine. I cry out in pain and finally collapse against the seat back, crying. I'm finally in.

Good Vibrations—NOT!

I'm so sensitive to vibrations that every bump feels like a major league baseball player is hitting my back full strength with a bat full of nails poking out. Do you know how many bumps there are in the road? Thousands!!! And every single one of them is excruciating! I'm trying not to scream out in pain while Eley is driving, because I don't want to upset her more. I can tell that she is really worried about me, and I don't want to cause her more grief, but when we hit some of the bigger bumps, I just can't help myself. The pain and reverberation are too much, and I just start crying. When she turns a corner, I have to push my knees together because I can't tolerate my body rocking back and forth around the corner. I am in so much pain, I just want her to stop the car and let me catch my breath. But we'd be stopping every minute, and that would only delay the agony.

Eley tells me that she is going to take notes while the doctor is speaking, so that we can both refer to them later … oh, my God, do we HAVE to turn another corner? Wait, I have to grab both knees and push them tightly together because, if I don't, it's like a hot branding iron is piercing my spine. I close my eyes because, otherwise, I will get dizzy. Okay, catch your breath, I tell myself. Just breathe. Just breathe. She's driving straight now. Good, okay; oh hell, a ramp??? We have to take the on-ramp to get onto the highway… Oh wait, please, I'm still dizzy from going around the corner, and now you want to go on a ramp? Now I'm starting to feel nauseous.

I look down to check if my arms are on fire, because they are burning. I expect to see smoke, but there is only the sun on my arms. I don't even have the window open, but the sun is scorching my arms. It's the synthetic marijuana that I'm on, causing that reaction. I ask Eley if she can reach my jacket that is in the back seat, and I drape it over my arms to put out the fire.

I think to myself, *why is Eley following so closely behind that car? Geez, slow down, you're almost in their back seat.* I'm slamming on my imaginary set of brakes on my side of the car, but it's not helping! Eley reassures me with gentleness that we are more than 3 car lengths away from that car, but it doesn't seem that way to me! When she finally stops the car and parks, I exhale a big breath of relief. We have finally stopped moving … no more bumps … but now Eley has to help me out of the car and into the doctor's office.

My Initial Consultation with Dr. Eileen Groves

Once inside the doctor's office, we are escorted to an exam room. I realize that it's taken me 1½ hours to get to this point, which only leaves me with 30 minutes of awake time. My "window of consciousness" is quickly closing, and I'm afraid I won't be able to stay awake much longer. I know Eley will be paying attention and taking notes during this first consultation because my short-term memory is foggy, at best. I am so exhausted that I just want to go home and crawl into bed. But without seeing this doctor, I have run out of options.

Luckily, the door opens and in she walks. Dr. Groves is a general practitioner and a craniosacral specialist who comes highly recommended. Since I am off work due to my back issues, I am hoping … actually praying … that she can help me.

With an outstretched hand that then meets mine, she smiles and says, "Hi, I'm Eileen." My first thought is, *she seems nice*.

Eileen starts by asking me why I've come to see her. Between Eley and me, we explain my unique situation. While taking notes, she then asks, "So are you taking any medication?" I reply, "Oh, yes." I hand her my list of all my medications and details of the daily dosages.

- OxyContin – 400 mg
- Oxy IR – 10 mg every 6 hours
- Ketamine – 1 mg up to 4 mg
- Cesamet – .05 mg – .10 mg
- Clonazepam – 2 pills nightly
- Lyrica – 600 mg
- Celebrex – 400 mg
- Percocet – 10 mg when needed

- (Plus 5 other pills to manage the side effects from these)

My list includes 13 different types of medications, 5 of which are narcotics. You probably recognize one of them: OxyContin??? Ring a bell? Yes, that's the drug that so many people are addicted to and are dying from on a daily basis. And I'm on **400 mg of it DAILY.** To put that amount into perspective, an initial prescription would be 5 or 10 mg, with the normal maximum daily dosage being 40 mg, which makes most people's heads spin. I am on 10 times that amount. Crazy, right?

OXY IR is a fast-acting form of the OxyContin, and I only take those when the pain is super intense, which is at least once a day. Clonazepam, a seizure medication and tranquilizer, has been prescribed for me to consume at night to try to calm down my restless leg syndrome and possibly, to help me sleep.

The final narcotic on that list is ketamine, which is used to tranquilize HORSES!!!!! To tranquilize a 1000-pound horse, a veterinarian would administer 2 mg. I am taking 4 mg daily … and I don't weigh anything near 1000 pounds.

She looks at me in disbelief, and asks me, "Who put you on all this stuff?" And I reply, "The pain killers were prescribed by a pain specialist," to which she replies, "What was she thinking? She should be shot! These narcotic dosages are enough to take down an elephant!" She then looks me straight in the eyes and says, "It's a miracle you are still alive."

Eileen stated that she has never had a patient on so many drugs and such large amounts of narcotics, in her entire practice. I guess I get the "Patient on the Most Drugs and Still Living" award.

Since I am leaning against the examination table, she begins to check my mobility and flexibility while I'm standing. She asks, "Can you bend forward and try to touch your toes?"

"Yes, I can do that," I reply. *Okay, that was easy,* I think to myself. "Now," Eileen asks, "come back up." I'm thinking, *okay, this is where it gets tricky.* I get about halfway up and feel my back tighten. I can't straighten up without grabbing the bed. You know those "level changes"—getting in or out of a chair, or on or off a toilet seat, which you do with ease—those are torture for me. It feels like a giant grabs my lower back and crushes it when I get about halfway. It's quite evident to Eileen that there is a major problem there.

"Lizzy, could you please lie down on the examination bed." *Now this,* I think to myself, *is going to be tricky.* It's another level change, with a complication. While going from standing to sitting is difficult, I have to be careful how I get my legs onto the bed. If my legs don't get on the bed together in one fell swoop, I will get a back spasm. From a sitting position, I push my knees together and lie down on my right side, making sure my feet get up on the bed. Then I roll my torso so that my back is flat on the bed, and my legs follow together, while I hold my knees with my hands. I can't lie on my back with my legs flat, so I ask Eileen for a pillow to put under them. After all that, she can now begin her assessment, starting right from the tip of my head. She doesn't find any areas that are of concern while I'm on my back.

"Can you roll over onto your stomach?" Oh boy. The part that I've been dreading is now about to start. Anyone touching my back is painful, but examining my back and pushing on different areas, that's excruciating … and she is barely touching me. "Eileen, I cut off the backs of my t-shirts because the weight of the material on my back causes me too much pain. I know that you have to touch my back, but I really don't want you to. So, if I hit you, it's just a defensive move to try to get your hand off of my back. I'm really sorry, but it's a reflex of mine now."

And hit her, I do. When she touches THOSE parts of my lower back, I scream, loudly. It's like being sucker punched but in your back, and of course, you can't see it coming. I am like a warrior waiting for the next strike. I know that it's coming, but I don't know from where. I am so hypersensitive that a wind blowing against my back causes me extreme pain. When someone actually TOUCHES my back, it feels like a sledge hammer has hit me. While logically I KNOW she isn't hitting me, it FEELS like she is. And Eileen is really thorough, which means she is touching my back A LOT!!!! I just wish I could take my back off and she could examine it without me being attached!!!

Finally, she asks me to sit up on the bed so that she can explain her findings. I let out a big sigh. The exam part is over!!! As I sit up with help, I realize just how tired I am. It took a lot of energy when she was examining me, because I didn't want her to touch my back. I was on guard the entire time.

Eileen begins to speak, but I can't understand what she is saying. I mean, I can see her lips moving, and I can hear the intonation of her words, but I can't comprehend a single word she is saying. I know that I should be paying attention here, but I am beyond tired. I mean, I can HEAR her; I just can't UNDERSTAND her. Of course, I can hear my internal "stay awake" timer ticking down.

So, I gently interrupt her and ask, "Can I lie down while you talk?" "Sure," Eileen replies. As I lie back down, I just keep thinking that Eley will take notes and ask all the right questions. With that internal dialogue convincing me that I am in safe hands, I fall asleep almost instantly, right there on her examination table.

Narcotics Cause Pain?

So, while I was sleeping…

The first thing Eileen tells Eley: "We need to get her off all of these narcotics." Eley is shocked, because I am in such pain and I need them for pain relief. I think I heard Eley saying, "But you don't understand how much PAIN she is in! If you decrease the meds, how is that going to help her? She'll just be in MORE pain!!"

Eileen then replies, "The reason Lizzy is having so much pain is that the massive amounts of narcotics are actually CAUSING some of the pain." Eileen goes on to explain that narcotics, up to a certain dosage, are beneficial in providing pain control;

however, past that dosage, they actually CAUSE pain. That is the point I am at. Just by decreasing the narcotics, I should be in less pain.

Another reason to decrease all these narcotics is that they could be masking other serious health concerns. As Eileen explained, I could be having serious health issues in other areas of my body that I may not even be aware of, because the narcotics are dulling those pain receptors.

But the most serious side effect from taking all of these drugs is that I could overdose, go into respiratory distress, and die.

I feel Eley gently touch my arm to wake me, and she says, "C'mon, it's time to go home." Eileen and Eley both help me off the bed. I feel so weak that they have to help me walk to the car. I painfully get in the front seat, and Eley helps me get my seat belt on. Eley is prepared. She has a blanket and tucks me in while putting a pillow under my head. Now we can make the long drive home.

I was asking Eley as she was driving, "So what did Dr. Eileen say?" Eley replied, "She wants to get you off all these drugs." And all I'm thinking is, *what does she mean she wants to get me off the pills?? Doesn't she know I'm in pain all the time!! How am I supposed to function if she takes away the pain pills?* But then Eley explains that the pills are causing pain. Okay, now I'm really confused. And to boot, Eley informs me that some narcotics, like OxyContin, cannot be stopped cold turkey as it would kill me. I will have to be weaned off of them slowly, so that my body can adjust to the decrease properly and safely.

Now I'm thinking, *how long is that going to take? And what do I do to control the pain while I'm weaning off of them? And how the heck am I supposed to figure all this out?*

In order to understand my confusion about the next steps, you have to understand what I was like BEFORE I got sick.

Chapter 2

My Life Before Narcotics

Can I be honest with you?

There is something quite unique about me. I was born in a litter. No, seriously. I am the oldest in a set of triplets! I'm an identical twin with my sister, Eley, and fraternal triplet with my brother, Eddie. Pretty neat, eh?

We were a bit of a surprise for our parents, to say the least. There were no fertility treatments available way back then (I'm aging myself) and no ultrasound either. My mom and dad already had my brothers: Ziggy, age 9, and Ronnie, age 4. By the time Mom was 3 months pregnant with us, she couldn't see her own feet! When the doctor listened to her belly with his stethoscope, he heard two distinct heartbeats, so he presumed there were two babies. He didn't know that Eley and I were rocking to the same beat. In the doctor's defense, triplets were very rare back then. The day my mom went into the hospital to be induced, they took an x-ray, and voila, they saw all three of us!

I grew up on a 150-acre dairy farm in Copetown, Ontario, which is about an hour west of Toronto. It's not a huge town, but it was a very close-knit community of farmers with strong work ethics.

I feel I had the best parents in the world. My dad was a Polish immigrant and a very strong, hardworking, kind man. I can count on one hand the number of times I saw my dad sick, because the cows had to be milked twice a day. He only had 7 weeks of holidays in 45 years; for him, farming was his passion. My mom's reputation for preparing the most delicious meals was well known, and she was such a wonderful, caring woman and mother. She worked hard every day and made our house a home.

My dad didn't believe that women should work in the barn around the cows (have I told you how much I loved my dad?), so my brothers, along with my dad, would milk the cows. Eley and I would help my mom with the household duties and outside lawn stuff. We all knew that we were a solid unit, and each of us contributed to keeping our family business running smoothly. There was always something that had to be done on the farm, and we learned how to drive tractors and pitch bales when required. I had an amazingly happy childhood, with a playground that stretched for 150 acres. Both of my parents were generous with encouragement, hugs, and love. I really feel blessed to have grown up with them by my side.

Looking back, I can't believe how healthy and strong both of my parents were. They worked hard every day to provide for the 5 of us, and while we weren't wealthy financially, we had happiness, great food, and love in abundance. If someone got sick, everyone else in the family would pitch in to help where it was required. Other than each of us kids breaking a limb or a nose, we were fairly healthy too, so aspirins were kept on hand just in case. If you had a bad cold, Mom, the one-glass-of-wine-per-year lady, would make a "hot toddy," with enough whiskey in it to grow hair on your chest! If we needed to see a doctor, we did. We rested until we were healthy again, and continued on.

What Drugs?

I never experimented with drugs in my youth as they really didn't interest me. Honestly, I've never even tried marijuana in any form (other than a synthetic marijuana that was prescribed later). I was certainly exposed to marijuana during my university days, but I stayed away from it. In regard to the "harder" drugs, like crack or heroin, I honestly have never seen them "in person." I know you can buy them on the street, but I'm so naïve that I don't even know what street that is!

Now, like most of society, alcohol was socially acceptable. I was able to drink alcohol in the Polish hall, long before I was of legal age (19 in Canada), but it was limited. I spent years as an active member of the PCAY (Polish Canadian Association of Youth) and had a large circle of friends. We spent almost every weekend together, going to polka dances and outings. We had members from Windsor to Toronto, so we travelled a lot. A couple of times a year, we even went to the States for festivals, during which we danced and drank. Anyone who knows me, knows that I LOVE, LOVE, LOVE to dance!!! As I got older, my alcohol tolerance really increased, but I never drank alone, never drank daily, and I **never** drink and drive. Alcohol was for social outings with my friends or family, and nothing that I have ever had a problem with.

Before I hurt my back, the strongest drug I had in my medicine chest was aspirin. I've been told that I have a very high pain tolerance, and feel like I can handle a bit of pain. When my dentist has to fill a cavity, I don't get freezing in my mouth. I can handle dental work quite well without the numbing agent. Overall, other than a few instances of strep throat, and removal of my appendix, my health was great.

The Working World

Shortly after graduating from the University of Western Ontario, in London, Ontario, I starting working full time for the Government of Canada. I was a bilingual client service representative at the call centre for unemployment insurance (U.I.), as it was called back then. I was the person who replied to the question, "Where's my cheque?" Yup, that was me. I was transferred to the local office in downtown Hamilton for a 6-

month assignment, and boy, did this little country bumpkin ever grow up quickly. The office was in a rougher part of downtown and brought in all types of people for the U.I. claims and employment services. I certainly learned to deal with all sorts people, and grew a thicker skin.

After transferring back to the non-public office, I worked as an agent assessing the unemployment insurance claims, which was a nice change. It was while I was working that job that a temporary assignment was posted to test software programs in Ottawa, our nation's capital. I was looking for a change and jumped at the chance to try something new. But did I forget to mention that the assignment was for 4 months—from February to May, the dead of winter—in Ottawa!

For those of you who are unfamiliar with Ottawa, let me give you a few details. The weather can fluctuate from -40 Celsius (-40 F) in the winter, to 40 Celsius (100 degrees F) in the summer. In February, Ottawa usually gets a cold snap of -40 C or colder, for at least two weeks. Cars that aren't plugged in normally won't start, and your nostrils freeze when you walk outside in that cold. The first snow usually begins in October and **does not melt** until mid-May. They have a 7.5 km (4.6 mile) long canal on which you can skate in the winter time, and where they host their Winterlude Festival. Spring feels like it only lasts for 2 weeks, with the Tulip Festival starting it off, and then summer settles in with killer humidity. I'm convinced that the early settlers didn't even have time to thaw and enjoy the warm weather before the cold and snow began again. That's why Ottawa was chosen as our nation's capital—the weather was awful, which they reasoned would deter the enemy from invading!

So, my first drive to Ottawa, to start my assignment, should have been an indicator of the weather in the months to come. Since we lived out in the country on the farm, we didn't have cable or the weather network. When I left Copetown that clear winter day, I unknowingly drove right into the path of a snowstorm. The journey should have taken me about 5½ hours, but it took me 7 hours—the first day. There was so much snow that they closed—yes, closed—a major highway: Hwy 401 at Brockville, while I was on it. I guesstimated where the exit ramp was and managed to find a hotel. The next day, I still had 110 km (60 miles) to go before I would reach Ottawa. Even with the snow plows actively clearing the highways, it still took me another 4 hours to get there.

I had never seen so much snow in my life. I mean, we get snow in Copetown, but this was Ottawa, which is much farther north. During the next 9 weeks of my assignment, we got 9 more snowstorms, dropping at least 30 cm (1 foot) of snow per snowstorm. It was crazy. They were removing the snow from the downtown core by the truckload, so that people could still park on the street.

But, oh, the first time I saw all the skaters on the canal, bundled up in their parkas and snowsuits enjoying Winterlude, I was hooked. Ottawa residents know that winter is going to be long, so they dress warmly and play outside!!!! There were at least 6 ski hills within a 20-minute drive from downtown, and I visited them all. What a winter wonderland!!!! And if you're lucky, you can warm up with a cup of hot chocolate and a Beavertail après-ski!!!

So, flash forwarding a year, I had finished my assignment and was working in Hamilton as an agent. One year later, they had another assignment, for 3 months in Ottawa again; but this time, it was for the summer months. I applied and found myself back in the capital; but this time, instead of a sea of white snow, there was landscaping … and grass … and parks … and a man-made lake that you could boat on!!! It was beautiful and fun. So many festivals and concerts are held that you don't have time to be bored. I ended up making friends with some of the other testers and had quite a busy social calendar. The majority of the testers were from Newfoundland, our most eastern province and island, and we just clicked. They were hard workers who loved to have fun, and I felt that I fit right in, even if I was a Mainlander (one who lives in the larger land mass of Canada).

Let's Get Physical

In Ottawa, the parkways are closed on Sunday mornings from May to September, to allow people to rollerblade, run, and walk on these beautifully paved streets. Each Sunday, we would meet to rollerblade and then head downtown for a bite to eat. My friends and I also played baseball on Thursday nights in a recreational league. The team was a mix of guys and girls, and although I wasn't a phenomenal baseball player, I was a girl … and we were often short of them on Thursday nights.

On Tuesday nights, I played volleyball with a group from work, and that was fun as well.

While on assignment, I applied as a Testing Analyst for a one-year period. After 6 months, they made my position permanent, which meant I was staying in Ottawa. After 3 years, I became a Team Leader, overseeing a group of 9 software testers. We tested various programs like Employment Insurance (its current name), Labour Programs, and mobile apps for onsite emergency response situations, like train derailments. I really liked my job. It was interesting, ever changing, and allowed me to have a career path that would have extended upward. My manager, Marcel, was a fabulous mentor, and I was hoping to apply for his job when he retired.

Break in Reality

Never in my wildest dreams would I have thought that after a back injury, I'd **never** be back at that desk again. The staff in that office, in which I worked Monday to Friday for 11 years, would change, and no one would know me. My name plate would have been removed long ago, and like me, would never return. All because of one little pill.

But really, how bad could it be to find out what is wrong? I have back pain, like millions of other people. There are treatments available, physical therapies, and medications to help ease the pain. How hard could it be to get better? Easy peasy, right? I never realized just how long and hard this journey was going to be.

Chapter 3

Let the Back Spasms Begin

My Hunt for a Diagnosis

This wasn't the first time I had back pain, so I wasn't really that concerned at first when I was off for 2 weeks on sick leave from work. I knew that the pain medication would help me handle the pain, and the anti-inflammatory practices (applying ice, topical creams, and taking Naproxen) would reduce the swelling, which would ultimately reduce the pain as well.

I had followed the same treatment plan when I was off before, in September of 2000, after I had hurt my back while doing some landscaping in the front yard of my house in Orleans. There was a cedar bush on each side of my front step, and the one on the right was dead. So, on a beautiful Sunday afternoon, I grabbed a shovel and started digging it out. When I thought I had hacked through all of the roots, I pulled the bush … and it pulled back … and then I heard a snap in my lower back. I knew instantly that something was terribly wrong. I slowly and very carefully made my way into the house and lay down on the couch in the living room. I was in so much pain that I didn't want to move an inch, because I would get spasms in my back. I had never had spasms before, but I knew I didn't like them when they hit! The next day, with the help of a friend, I made it to my doctor's office for a consultation and a plan of treatment. After 2 weeks, I returned to work as expected.

But this time, in February 2005, it was completely different. Although I saw my doctor and took the prescribed pain medications as directed, I still could barely function after 2 weeks. Another visit to my doctor provided me with a second set of narcotics and another 2 weeks off. *Certainly, after this, my life would return to normal*, I thought. Nope.

I was just as stumped as my family doctor. I consider myself to be pretty stoic, with a fairly high pain tolerance. But this pain was unlike anything I had experienced before. To be honest, it scared me. When the spasms hit, they would put me on the floor, writhing in pain, with A LOT of four-letter words coming out of my mouth. That behaviour was very unlike me; but truthfully, no other words seemed to be as suitable to the situation as those swear words.

At this time, in 2005, the overall assumption for resolving back pain was to rest. Personally, I really couldn't do anything else. A normal, reasonable person would have sat down, because the pain would prevent them from wanting to do anything else. However, after 4 weeks, my doctor and I thought physiotherapy might help in easing tight muscles and the spasms. The first few visits, I was shown simple stretches that I could do with the utmost care and concern. You have to remember, I was scared of moving, so stretching wasn't something I felt comfortable doing. But with the physiotherapist's help, I found I could move more, without a spasm, if I concentrated on HOW I was moving. The biggest issue was what I called level changes: going from a sitting to a standing position (and vice versa)— bending at the waist was fine when going down to touch my toes, but coming back up was excruciating. I even tried the treadmill for extra movement, but after 5 minutes at a very low speed level, my back couldn't handle it anymore. The cramping would begin and that would be enough for me, forcing me to stop.

At the same time, I was doubting how I was going to handle returning to work. Although I lived in Orleans, one of the eastern suburbs of Ottawa, I worked in Hull, Quebec, in a massive government complex that housed 21,000 people, in Place du Portage. Just to get from the bus stop to my desk, it was about a 10-minute walk, so how was I supposed to do THAT? I could barely stroll on a treadmill for 5 minutes!

One thing that most people don't realize is how exhausting being in pain really is. Our body's normal state is one of health and ease; however, when you get sick, it becomes a state of disease, and often pain. My back spasms were essentially trauma to my system, and being in constant pain made my body fight, in addition to doing what it had to do to keep me functioning. In addition to those spasms, I was experiencing a temporary "restless leg syndrome," which for me usually occurred when I was trying to fall asleep. This is a fairly common syndrome, where my legs would randomly "jump," causing me to be startled awake. It wasn't fun, especially with my back being so sensitive to vibrations.

During my sessions with the physiotherapy, it became apparent that although I was stretching better, I wasn't progressing as well as they had hoped. A new modality was suggested, and that was intramuscular stimulation (IMS). It involves inserting a needle into a muscle, which causes the muscle to "grab" the needle and then release it. So picture this: They are inserting this acupuncture needle right into my muscles that keep spasming, so that it will spasm again in order to make it relax. Oh yeah, it hurt ... A LOT!!! The very first needle, which was completely straight that they put into my back, came out with a 90-degree bend. When your physiotherapist says, "Wow, I've never seen THAT happen before!" you know it's not a good omen. And I had about 15 needles each time I went. It was so painful. I cried like a baby. I mean, imagine having a muscle cramp in your calf that would spasm 10–15 times a day, and THEN have someone insert a needle into that same muscle. And the worst part was that it didn't help.

But I kept searching with the help of my family doctor. I had CAT scans, MRIs, and nerve blocks. Then one of the specialists suggested that I get Botox. No, not in my face; in my back! Botox is a neurotoxin and works by attaching itself to nerve endings; and it relaxes, not freezes, the muscles. I was told that several injections would be put directly into my muscles and the surrounding muscles to prevent the constant spasming. At a cost of $375 Canadian per vial, which was not covered by our OHIP (Ontario Health Insurance Plan), I was told I would need to order 2 Botox vials and bring them with me to my procedure. It was an expensive afternoon.

My sister, Eley, drove me to Hamilton for the treatment, and she witnessed the treatment procedure, which she equated to watching a loved one being tortured. Man, did I ever swear during that procedure. Of course, I apologized right after each swear word used, and then, of course, cried uncontrollably. It was incredibly painful, much more than I had anticipated. While it worked on the muscles that received the Botox, other muscles seemed to clue in and started spasming. Botox felt like a million needles, but I know logically that it was about only 20 injections.

After a few months, in February 2006, this same specialist felt that the mechanical back pain I was having could be helped by injecting Botox again, but this time into specific facet joints in my spine, in a procedure called a medial branch nerve block. The doctor felt that the nerves were a major part of my pain, so he gave me a prescription to pick up 3 vials (of 100 mg each) of Botox this time. He booked the procedure room for using fluoroscopy, so he was able to guide the needle into the correct region of my back. That wasn't a lot of fun because he assaulted the majority of my spine with those injections. Remember, with my hypersensitivity and overall pain I was feeling, this was torture … again. It was the last Botox treatment I ever had, but on a happy note, my back has no wrinkles!

1200 Needles and Counting

Now, I realize that there are some individuals who are absolutely terrified of needles. Personally, I really don't like having needles in my mouth. I prefer to have dental fillings done without freezing, as I can tolerate the drill and a little pain if required. Otherwise, I don't mind getting needles when required. I guess that's a good thing, considering that during my search for a diagnosis, I've had several treatments that required many, many needles.

The first was during my physiotherapy. After following the list of suggested exercises, and having ultrasound treatments, the physiotherapist suggested that I try IMS, the intramuscular stimulation that I detailed earlier. I had IMS treatments for months, which required about 12 needles per sitting, so that is a few hundred there.

I had never heard of prolotherapy treatment, but it was suggested by one of the many specialists I had seen. The procedure is simply to inject a saline solution into the soft tissue, in the area of concern (typically around a joint), to invoke an inflammatory response, forcing the body to heal the ligaments and tendons. It is also known as a regenerative joint injection, or non-surgical ligament and tendon reconstruction.

After meeting with the specialist, my treatment plan was to include 8 prolotherapy sessions on my lower back, which would involve approximately 12 injection sites. I was required to attend all 8 sessions, or the treatment would be deemed inconclusive. I thought I might as well try this as it just might be the answer I've been searching for.

While the doctor was professional and very knowledgeable, the treatments were extremely painful. My back was so hypersensitive that wind passing over my back would make me cry out in pain. In fact, I used to cut the backs off of my t-shirts because the weight of the material was too painful. So injecting anything into my back was brutal. Plus, you can't SEE what's happening. While the doctor may tell you that he's about to inject it, it was still traumatic for me.

Leaving the doctor's office, I would be a mess. I can't even begin to explain how awful I felt. One of my dear friends, Pablo, had offered to drive me to and from my appointments, and I don't know how he handled me crying so well. After each session, I would get into his car and explode into tears. I remember, after the 6th session, I told him and Gemma, his wife, who I worked with, that I wasn't going back there. I just couldn't go through that pain again. While the injections weren't fun, it was my body's response—the inflammation effect—that was so excruciating. With 12 areas now angry and inflamed, it was more than I could bear. They spent the entire ride home convincing me to return for the final 2 treatments. They kept telling me, "What if those are the ones that make the pain go away?" I knew they were right. I agreed to attend those final 2 sessions. Unfortunately, there was no change to my pain level after the 8th session, and the doctor felt that no more could be done in his office for me.

Then acupuncture, a bone scan, medial branch nerve blocks, nerve tests, a myelogram (to check for cysts or tumors on my spine), and countless other tests just kept adding to the total. And after all that, I just couldn't understand why I couldn't find a doctor who could give me a definitive diagnosis. With all of the technological advances in medicine, it was baffling to me why tests would yield no further answers. At least I didn't have to have multiple invasive surgeries to get the same diagnostic results. However, it was so depressing when the test would come back negative, and the doctor would tell me that in his or her field of expertise, I was just fine. I was waiting for the line, "It must be all in your head," but thankfully, I never got that answer. I KNEW that something horrible was going on, but it was anyone's guess as to what. I thought, *how many doctors and specialists do I have to see before SOMEONE, ANYONE, has an answer!!!*

Can Anyone Help Me?

I was on a real mission! To find someone, ANYONE, who could find out what was wrong with my back! Then with their help or others, I could get the issue fixed and return to a "normal" life. With my family doctor's help, I saw rheumatoid arthritis specialists, chiropractors, neurologists, and even a physiatrist, which is a doctor who specializes in physical medicine and rehabilitation for those whose daily functioning has been impaired.

I thank God that I live in Canada, where we have universal health care. Without getting into the specifics, basically anyone who lives in Canada gets the medical care or emergency care that they require. We have the same level of service, whether you are unemployed or a millionaire. Obviously, some procedures (for example, cosmetic) would have to be paid out of pocket, and we may wait longer for a procedure, but we aren't forced to pay up front for medical services. We have provincial and territorial health plans (like OHIP for Ontario residents), and even agreements between provinces. Unlike our nearest neighbouring country, the United States, no one is without health care in Canada. It is funded through our taxes, so we do PAY for it; we just don't get a physical bill when we leave the hospital or doctor's office in most cases.

And to that I say, thank God. I can't even begin to calculate what must have been spent on my particular case. With all of the doctors, specialists, health care professionals, tests, MRIs, nerve blocks, and all the rest, I don't even know what the dollar value would have been. But I was desperate for an answer. I just couldn't accept that there was no reasonable explanation for the back pain I was experiencing! Surely SOMEONE could find out what was happening and help me return to my previous life. It was so frustrating and depressing when test after test came back negative. While I was getting an "answer," it became more a game of elimination than the answer I was waiting for. Sometimes that answer was a remedy to try this or that treatment (using ice on my back, more stretching, etc.), or sometimes it was a pill, like an anti-inflammatory. But there was no resolution, and it was so disheartening. I felt I had a treatable medical condition that no one could name. I mean, how hard could it be to find the answer?

While my family doctor, who I trusted explicitly, was trying to manage my increasing pain to the best of her knowledge, it became quite apparent that we had to look at another option. Finally, after seeing over 50 doctors—yes, that number is correct—my family doctor suggested I see a pain specialist. The pain specialist would review my case and put me on a drug regimen that would allow me some relief while we continued to search for the root cause of my back pain. The pain specialist's forte was their knowledge of which drugs worked well together to deal with such unusually severe pain. At this point, I was willing to have another doctor review my meds to see what they would suggest. I just wanted my life to return to normal, and to go back to functioning like a healthy individual. Little did I know how far I was yet to fall.

Chapter 4

Meeting My Drug Dealer—Oops, I Mean Pain Specialist

I really felt lucky that day, after learning that a new pain clinic was opening up in the Ottawa area, and I only had to wait 3 months instead of years to see a pain specialist. This was the first time I had felt hope in a very long time. My family doctor felt it was in my best interest to get my pain under control while we searched endlessly for a diagnosis.

After the three months elapsed, I found myself waiting to meet this pain specialist. From my research, I had learned that she was an anesthesiologist. This would require an individual becoming a doctor and then spending 4 years in the specialty of anesthesiology. Since these very specialized doctors are the ones who administer the drugs before and during surgery, while monitoring our every breath, they play a very important role and have a great deal of responsibility. We are truly putting our lives in their hands during surgery.

Anyone who has dealt with chronic pain knows that living with constant severe pain is absolutely exhausting. The body has so much pain to deal with that it uses all available energy trying to get it under control. You don't have the energy that you need to do most of the basic day-to-day activities, and being sociable is a really exhausting chore. Most people find that their voices grow weaker, as they lack the energy required to project their voice as they once did. It is a constant struggle just to get through the day. You tire easily and life isn't any fun.

Before I continue, I want to underline the fact that I will be calling my pain specialist "Dr. X," as I don't really feel the need to expose her in my book. She is just one of hundreds of doctors who continue to **overprescribe** dangerously addictive drugs, like OxyContin, to millions of people daily. I'm not sure how much money doctors receive as a kickback for prescribing certain drugs, but I know that the pharmaceutical company, Purdue, that makes OxyContin, was making hundreds of millions of dollars during this time just by producing and selling **this one drug**. While Purdue has since been found guilty of misleading doctors by not revealing exactly how addictive OxyContin really is, there were still hundreds of doctors who found it so easy to keep filling their patients' pockets with prescriptions.

There are systems in place to review how many narcotics are being prescribed by a certain doctor, which some have labelled the "narcotic police." In some cases, the amount of Oxy-Contin being prescribed was, to put it lightly, excessive. In some cases, small town doctors were prescribing more OxyContin in a month than multiple doctors in the largest cities in Canada and the United States. Once the word was out that a certain doctor would prescribe OxyContin without even examining a new patient or an existing one, the temptation became too easy to over-prescribe.

Let's Chat

When the day arrived for my pain specialist appointment, I had a mix of emotions, but hope was the strongest. After seeing so many medical professionals who could not offer any answers, I was praying that my constant severe pain could be controlled so that I could return to a normal life. I made sure to take my list of medications with me, and the physical bottles as well, just in case I couldn't keep them straight.

When I met with Dr. X, I was on 160 mg of OxyContin daily, Oxy IR for breakthrough pain, and a pill at night to calm me, all of which she reviewed. I told her about the constant pain, back spasms, lack of energy, and my previous and current back injury. I informed her that after seeing over 50 different doctors, I was still without a diagnosis. I had tried all sorts of therapies, such as physiotherapy, chiropractic therapies, nerve blocks, IMS (inter-muscular stimulation therapy), and prolotherapy, with little success. I told her that I just couldn't understand why no one could find the issue. I had had x-rays, CAT scans, blood work, and any other test doctors suggested, but all of the results came back as "negative." "Negative" is usually an excellent result in the medical world. However, for me, it meant that while we were able to rule out what I "didn't" have, we had no answer to what I did have.

While discussing the medications I was on, I also raised my concern about the side effects of several of them. Weight gain was the most obvious side effect of Lyrica, one of the new drugs that I was taking. I had gained 50 pounds—yes, 5-0—while being off on sick leave. While I realized that I wasn't moving as much as when I was healthy, I couldn't understand how I had gained that much weight. I know I wasn't eating the greatest, but 50 pounds is a HUGE gain. I knew that carrying more weight on my frame was hard on my already stressed back. She suggested that this drug was probably slowing my metabolic rate so that I wasn't burning as many calories; hence, I was storing the excess as fat.

She suggested a couple of options after reviewing the documentation that had been forwarded from my doctor, and from information I provided verbally. With my back spasms continuing for days on end, she felt that my body was, for lack of a better term, "stuck in a loop," where the spasms just kept repeating and didn't know when to stop. The first option was to increase my OxyContin by an additional 40 mg a day. I agreed because I felt she was the expert. I mean, really, who I am to question a specialist? I don't have any medical training, and I knew enough not to trust everything that Dr. "Google" or any other web page suggested. Plus, she had years of specialized training in drugs and anesthesia. She manipulated a few of my drugs, but the major change was the OxyContin amount. She added on an additional 40 mg a day, sharing that she felt I needed to control my pain level more.

The second suggestion she made was to have two epidurals, scheduled one week apart. She asked if I had ever had an epidural, and I replied that I hadn't. But I was rightly a little anxious about having one. She proceeded to detail the pros and cons of the procedure, and a risk could be paralysis if something went wrong. However, that risk was extremely low. She felt that by performing two epidurals a week apart, it would stop this loop that my body was in, sort of like a reset button for a computer. Hopefully, this would stop the horrific spasms I was getting and reduce my pain. After having tried everything under the sun up to this point, I was willing to schedule the first epidural for the following week in her office.

Epidural and the Fire Alarm

A week later, Pablo had driven me to my appointment, and I had talked his ear off the entire car ride because I was so scared. When we got to the clinic, he tried to calm me down. His voice was soothing while he patted my hand, letting me blab on about who knows what. I just needed to do something while I waited to be called in. When they came to lead me into the procedure room, Pablo stayed in the waiting room.

So there I was, dressed in only a hospital gown, sitting on an examination table and looking out of the third-floor window. I was checking out the activity in the parking lot in front of the medical building, trying to calm myself, knowing that I was getting an epidural in mere minutes. I was alone and cold. God, I was so scared. I didn't know a lot about epidurals, but I did know that there was real risk that I was one wrong needle poke away from paralysis. Dear God, not that yet! I was so nervous … actually, I was feeling every type of emotion: fear, dread, and a small amount of hope too. I was sweating from nerves and narcotics, waiting for Dr. X to arrive.

With a quick knock on the door, she entered the room. She seemed very relaxed, which was so opposite from what I was feeling. She kept reassuring me, and I tried to calm my breathing. With me hugging a pillow, she began to sterilize my back. While talking me through what she was doing, she inserted the needle and performed the epidural. After the procedure, she was cleaning up the supplies on the table when … the fire alarm went off! Yup, I'm serious, the fire alarm. So there I was, sitting, basically paralyzed from the waist down, and the fire alarm was blaring! She shook her head and said, "Just wait here; I'll see if it's a drill or not."

While she was gone, through the window, I saw the fire engine and ambulance drive into the parking lot. I thought, *Oh great, I'm going to have to drag myself out of here to get help!* She came back shortly after and said that it was a false alarm and that we had been given the "all clear." I chuckle about it now, because the timing was exquisite. I mean, what are the odds of having an epidural and then the fire alarm going off?? I should have bought a lotto ticket that day!

Driving

After leaving her office, I knew that my medications had been increased to a much stronger and dangerous level, so I made a life-changing decision: I stopped driving. I didn't cancel my license, but I didn't get behind the wheel of a vehicle again until I felt I was in control and could react quickly and confidently. Little did I know, that would be 4 ½ years later.

For anyone who has not driven for a while, you realize quickly that your independence is gone; you end up relying on

EVERYONE to do errands and to go to appointments. Prescriptions that were only a 4-minute drive away were now being delivered by a taxi to my home. You really do take for granted jumping into your car to go pick something up or run a quick errand. I now had to rely on my friends for the simplest things, as my family lived over 5 hours away.

What made it difficult was that my doctor visits and various therapies lasted for hours, so if my friends (otherwise known as my chauffeurs) weren't able to stay for the entire appointment, they would have to come back again to pick me up! I can't even calculate how much time my friends spent driving me and my hypersensitive back around, while I tried not to scream out with each painful vibration. I know how blessed I am to have had such incredible friends.

Increasing the Medications

After a month, I went in for my next appointment with the pain specialist so that we could assess my current health. Unfortunately, the epidural didn't make any difference in my pain or the spasms, so we just added that to the growing list of unsuccessful procedures.

After the increase of OxyContin she had prescribed last month, I told her that I was still in constant, excruciating pain. I really couldn't explain why, because I was taking the drugs as prescribed, including the extra 40mg a day of OxyContin. I told her I was so exhausted and foggy. It just didn't make sense to me that even after taking the extra dose daily, I was still not getting any relief.

She reviewed the notes she had made from my last visit and decided that she would increase the OxyContin again by another 40 mg daily. She hoped that it would get the pain under control and allow me to function better. I agreed and went home.

It wasn't until later that evening, when I called Eley to tell her the update, that I began to question the treatment plan. I mean, listen, I was taking a lot of medication, and my mind was fuzzy, to put it lightly. I just couldn't think clearly or quickly enough to question what the pain specialist had suggested. When Eley, almost yelling, said, "What do you mean she increased the Oxy-Contin AGAIN by another 40 mg?" It was the first time I actually questioned the pain specialist's decision.

ICU (Intensive Care Unit) Visit #1

A very cold day, in February 2007, started out as just another typical day for me, in my overly drugged state. I got up at about 9 a.m., and the first thing I did in the morning was call Eley to let her know I was okay and alive. You might think I'm trying to be funny, but that was the truth. We would talk to each other twice a day to check in because she needed to know I was okay, especially since we lived so far from each other.

After our call, I would feed my cats and play with them a bit with a feather toy that they would chase. I really felt guilty that I wasn't able to spend more "awake" time with them, but it was physically impossible to stay awake for more than a couple of hours a day. You know, when you are sleeping more than your cats, that's a problem!

I watched *The Ellen DeGeneres Show* during the week as my way of keeping up with current TV shows, events, and music. I couldn't watch movies or documentaries because I couldn't concentrate long enough to follow along with the plot or story line. At least with Ellen's show, she made me laugh, which truly is the best medicine. And if I was in my "giggly" state, I would laugh until my stomach hurt.

After having a bite to eat for breakfast, I lay down for a few hours. When I awoke at 5:30 p.m., I remember lying in my bed feeling really hot, in the middle of winter, in Canada. I mean, there was literally 4 feet of snow outside and my thermostat was still set to 22 degrees Celsius (72 degrees Fahrenheit), just like every other day. I kicked off the covers and was boiling. So I proceeded to strip my bed of all the blankets and sheets, and I lay back on the bare mattress to try to get cooler. That seemed to make perfect sense to me at the time, although I've never done it before or since. The bare mattress still felt like I was lying on a heating blanket, so what did I do? I went into my spare bedroom on the main floor and lay down on that bed. I was still too hot. So, I stripped THAT bed of everything and lay down on THAT bare mattress. I got the same result. I then went downstairs to my other bedroom and lay down on that bed. Again, I was roasting. And you guessed it: I stripped that mattress bare. I was still feeling too hot.

At this point, my cats, Cougie and Shyna, had been watching me and following me from bedroom to bedroom. All of the sheets and blankets were now on the bedroom floors, and I was squirming on the beds trying to get cool. I'm sure they were wondering what the heck I was doing as they had never seen this behaviour before. And you have to understand that with my back injury, I could barely move or bend, let alone strip three beds and squirm around on the mattresses.

I went back upstairs and got a cold glass of water. I remember looking at the clock on the stove; it was 6 p.m. I felt a twitch in my right shoulder, which felt really strange. It was an involuntary movement where my shoulder would lift up every 30 seconds or so. Since I was still overheating, I put an ice pack on my shoulder to try to stop the twitching. And that's all I remember … until 8 p.m., 2 hours later.

I found myself standing in the living room, but I couldn't remember how I got there. Both of my cats were staring at me with a look of total fright, but I didn't know why. I remember telling them that I was okay, but I probably didn't look that great. My shoulder was now twitching every 15 seconds, and now I felt like there were thousands of bugs crawling all over my body. It was so irritating, and it was making my back hurt even more. Then the phone rang. I went into the kitchen to answer it; it was my sister, Eley, checking in on me for the second time that day. I remember her asking me how I was feeling. By now, I was so agitated by this twitching and these "bugs" that I could barely hold the phone steady. I walked into my bedroom, threw the phone on the bed, and shouted out, "I can't talk to you right now!!! There are bugs crawling all over my body, and I can't stop the twitching!" And I hung up on her.

Poor Eley! She was about 5½ hours away from me and couldn't just drop in to check on me. Within seconds, she called me back. I answered the phone with an angry, "What??" and she replied, "You're probably having a drug reaction. You need to call someone to get you to the hospital. Call Theresa and then call me back." "Okay," I said, and I hung up again. Before Eley had said that I might be having a drug reaction, that thought had never crossed my mind. My brain was too busy trying to deal with the twitching and the bugs to try to think of anything else. Now I realized that I needed help.

I called Theresa, who lived about 10 minutes away, but she wasn't home; I got her answering machine. With the calmest voice I could muster, I left her a message to call me as soon as she got home, and I hung up. And then I was back to fighting off all these bugs. I remember doing some pretty painful grimaces and physical movements in an attempt to "shake off" these imaginary bugs—they were relentless, and nothing was working. And my back was screaming.

Eley called back and asked me if Theresa was on her way. I replied so calmly, "No, she wasn't home, so I just left her a message." I can still hear how matter-of-fact I was—so unbothered by that fact—but Eley was downright scared. She told me, "Listen, you call Gemma and Pablo right now, and ask them to drive you to the hospital."

Gemma and Pablo lived in Orleans as well, so when I called them, I told them that I thought I was having a drug reaction. They said they were on their way. I called Eley back and told her that I finally found a ride. She said, "Take your meds with you." I told her I would, and I hung up. That's when Eley started pacing. She was going out of her mind, 500 kilometres (310 miles) away. Eley is very knowledgeable about the body and medical procedures, and she knew the danger I was in. If my body had too many drugs in it, I could go into respiratory distress and stop breathing. There was a real possibility that I could die. While she was walking miles around her living room, she contemplated catching a flight to Ottawa. She would have to drive about 1¼ hours to Toronto, then wait for the hour-long flight, and then, once in Ottawa, try to find me. Or she thought that she could drive the 5 1/2 hours, so that she would at least have her car. But the winter roads were really bad that night, so she decided to stay put until she heard from me or Gemma.

Meanwhile, the voice inside my head kept telling me, "Take your meds, take your meds," but I just couldn't FIND them. I am a VERY organized person, and this was frustrating me—where did I put them? It took me 5 minutes to get my medicines and pill bottles, which were 10 feet away from me in a kitchen cupboard, into a plastic bag. Then I heard the banging on my door.

I know that they were not prepared for how I looked or acted when I opened the door. It was the middle of a snowy February in Orleans, Ontario, and Gemma and Pablo were dressed in their winter parkas and boots. When I opened the door, I was dressed in shorts and a t-shirt, covered in sweat, with an ice pack on my shoulder... Oh, and did I mention that the twitching of my right shoulder was now occurring every 15 seconds? I mustered a "Hi," and I saw absolute fear and concern in their eyes.

They had been to my home many times before today, and they knew that I am a very neat person who likes a clean home. They told me later that it looked like a cyclone had gone off in my house. There was bedding and pillows in the hallway and in the living room; the dry cat food was scattered on the kitchen floor, and the pillows from the couch were tossed all over the living room and dining room. Not to mention that I looked like a crazed person trying to get an imaginary enemy off of themselves. With their help, I managed to put on some pants, boots, and a jacket. I grabbed my purse from the hall closet and, with a new ice pack on my shoulder, they helped me walk to the car.

They decided to put me in the front passenger seat while Pablo drove. Gemma sat in the back, on the edge of her seat so that she could be closer to me. Even though I was in excruciating back pain, I was so irritated by all these "bugs" crawling all over me, that at several points during the journey, I remember vividly having **my feet on the inside roof of the car.** Pablo was driving like a maniac, going about 120 km an hour (70 miles an hour) on the highway to Riverside Hospital. Pablo had locked all the doors as they were afraid that I might fall out or, heaven forbid, open the car door and jump out of the car, trying to get the bugs off.

It was about 8:30 p.m. when we pulled into the Riverside Emergency Department, and it was dark. My heart sank. Gemma jumped out of the car and went into the hospital to see if they could see me, but the security guard told her that the emergency department was closed. He suggested we go to the General Hospital, which was only about 5 minutes away.

Meanwhile, Pablo and I were sitting in the car, and I was BEGGING him to let me out of the car so that he could RUN me over. I remember telling him vividly that I needed him to run over me with the car, repeatedly so that I could get out of this pain and agitation! He kept saying, "Lizzy, I can't do that!!!" And I re-assured him that I would set it straight with God so that it wouldn't be a murder. I just wanted the pain and the "hee-beegeebees" to end.

Gemma returned to the car with the new information, and we started driving again. Pablo got turned around and couldn't figure out how to get to the General Hospital. He was—how do I put it gently—directionally challenged. But even in my "state," I got us going in the right direction. At one point, I was so irritated that Gemma started rubbing my shoulder from the back seat while reciting the Lord's Prayer. We all started reciting it together.

Gemma and Pablo told me later that they thought I was having a stroke.

Once we got to the General, Gemma, this cute but slightly vertically challenged Filipino lady, jumped out of the car, grabbed a wheelchair from the entrance, ran back to the car, and helped me into it. Then, with me and my bags of meds in the wheelchair, she raced right into the nurse's station. I've never seen Gemma run so fast!!! She was probably thinking, *do something with her!!!*

Here I was, covered in sweat, with a now-thawed ice pack on my shoulder, in the middle of winter, holding 13 different bottles of medications, twitching every 15 seconds, and trying to hold back tears of pain and frustration. Oh, did I forget to mention that I kept yelling, "Get these bugs off of me!" while twitching uncontrollably.

I remember the nurse telling me to try to calm down. Calm down? Really? I AM CALM, except when there are bugs crawling all over me! She then asked me what meds I was taking. Even though I had a list of my meds in my purse, and a bag with all of them in my hands, I stared at the ceiling trying to remember what I was taking. And of course, I was still twitching. Finally, the nurse got all my info; she took my medications and told me to have a seat in the waiting room. I remember being shocked and thinking, *What? You want me to WAIT out there while I'm going through whatever THIS is?* But the thought was fleeting because the bugs were back, and I had to deal with them! I can just imagine what the nurses were thinking: *Oh, great, it's not even 9 p.m. on a Friday night, and the druggies have already started coming in!!*

Gemma wheeled me into the waiting room, where about 10 others were waiting to be seen. No one, and I mean NO ONE, would make eye contact with me, but they were obviously fascinated by my actions. Here I was, spasming and contorting like some fish out of water, and they knew they shouldn't stare at me, but they couldn't look away. I'm sure they had never seen anything or anyone like me before that night! Some of them even moved to seats that were farther away from me, hoping I wouldn't sit beside them.

It was only about a minute later when the nurse came out and called my name. Gemma and Pablo didn't even have a chance to sit down. She asked me if I could walk, and I replied yes. She told me, "Follow me." Within 15 seconds, I was in a private room with 2 nurses who were helping me undress while I leaned on them for support. They threw a gown on me and settled me into an ICU (intensive care unit) bed. They were hooking me up to an intravenous drip, monitors, and a blood pressure cuff. I was told that I was no longer allowed to walk on my own without a nurse helping me, and I was not to leave the bed. Then they put the rails up. I kept telling them it was time to take my meds, but they told me that until they figured out what was going on, they wouldn't allow me to take anything. I continued to writhe in pain; I was in such agony.

Once they got me all hooked up, I asked the nurses to tell Gemma and Pablo to go home, but they said I would have to tell them that myself. So, they ushered them in, and I begged them, "Please go home. It's going to be hours before they will discharge me, and I don't want you waiting here. They will take good care of me now, so please go home." I had already stressed them out enough. I didn't even realize how disheveled I must have looked, until Pablo gently pulled my gown down over my left thigh. With all of my wiggling, my gown had moved up a little bit to show about a half-inch of my underwear. He didn't want me to be embarrassed, so he fixed it for me.

Little did I know, when they left the hospital, they went back to my house to remake all the beds and straighten up the mess. They made sure that my cats had food and water, and then locked up my house. When they got to their house, they called Eley to let her know the latest. Eley had been anxiously waiting for an update, and while she appreciated their call, they really didn't have any answers for her.

Meanwhile, about 5 minutes later, the doctor came in to see

me and asked me all sorts of questions while I twitched along: How long had I been taking these meds? Did I take any extra pills tonight? Did I have any other conditions that they should know about? Had this ever happened before? Had I drunk any alcohol or taken any illegal drugs? "No, and I've NEVER taken an illegal drug in my life!!" I reassured them. But the most important question he asked was, "Who the hell put you on all these meds?" And I replied, "A pain specialist." He then replied, "Were they trying to kill you!! I'm surprised you haven't died from all of these pills." He admitted that he didn't really know what the reaction was caused by, but he suspected that it might be the OxyContin and a newer drug that I was also taking. I had just refilled my OxyContin prescription three days before. The doctor said that it wasn't an OxyContin overdose caused by me taking too many OxyContin pills, because they had counted the ones in the bottle to make sure.

I remember asking the doctor about this awful metallic smell that was so powerful in the room. "Can't you smell that?" "No," he replied. "Only YOU are smelling that." He said, "I'll be right back," and left the room. It was the first time I had seen one of the nurses wearing a pair of Crocs, and I thought the smell was coming from them. It was nasty.

The twitching and those bugs crawling all over me continued. I was sweating profusely, and the sheets and blanket on the bed were soaked. All the while, the medical team was trying to figure out what to do with me! They left me alone, and I started ripping all the sheets off the bed—while still being on it—as I was trying to cool down, just like I had done at home. Then I just started crying uncontrollably and shaking. I was all alone in the room, with millions of bugs crawling on me, and no one was helping me. I kept crying out, "Please, someone, HELP me!"

The nurse returned about 10 minutes later and told me she had a drug that hopefully would stop all of this twitching. She gave it to me intravenously and we waited. At first, we thought it worked, but the heebeegeebees returned within 30 seconds and were just as violent as before. I started to cry again. The two nurses kept trying to calm and soothe me by reminding me that there were now **two** very smart doctors on my case. Why couldn't they figure this out?

About an hour later, the neurologist on call came in to see me and injected a different drug into my IV, and the twitching finally stopped!!!! Wait … are they really stopping for good? Wait for it … YES!!! Oh, thank GOD!!!! It was 10:30 p.m. by then, and the feeling of relief was indescribable!!! It had been 4½ hours of relentless twitching, but now the "bugs" were finally gone. I was drenched and completely and utterly exhausted. Every muscle in my body ached, and my back was excruciatingly sore. Shortly thereafter, a nurse came in and gave me my pills that I should have taken 2 hours before. It took everything in my power just to lift my arm to grab the cup of water and take my pills. I had never been so exhausted like this in my life. Before I dozed off, the nurses put on fresh, dry linen and blankets on the bed, a fresh dry gown on me, and basically tucked me in. I thanked them profusely and was asleep within seconds.

The next thing I was aware of was being moved to a holding area, at about 7 a.m., while waiting for another neurologist to assess me, before I could be discharged. He made me walk back and forth, asked me a million questions, and said that my baby finger still had a tiny twitch in it. He really didn't know why I had gone through what I did, but he suspected it was some reaction between the drugs I was on. He didn't really know what caused it or if/when I would have another episode, but he said that if I continued on that many drugs, it was likely to happen again. He advised me to see my doctor about getting off of some of those drugs. Finally, he said he was going to discharge me at noon, and suggested I call a friend to take me home then.

My breakfast came and nothing tasted right. I had a hard-boiled egg that tasted like it had been boiled in 1947!! After one bite, I left the rest of it on the plate. Even the toast with grape jelly didn't taste right, not to mention the lukewarm coffee in the plastic cup. As a proud Canadian, I was missing my Tim Horton's coffee! Oh, and the metal smell was finally gone.

I phoned Eley and let her know I was still alive. Little did I know that Eley, Gemma, and Pablo had slept with their phones beside them all night, waiting for news. I then called Gemma and Pablo and asked if they could pick me up at noon. They asked if I had breakfast, and I replied, "Sort of." They promised me that we would stop at Tim Hortons on the way home to get a coffee that tasted like coffee, and anything else I wanted. God love 'em!!

When I finally got home, my furry babies were so excited to see me. My house looked perfectly put together, and I was so grateful to God for my wonderful friends and sister who got me through that episode, as well as the nurses and doctors who persevered to find a solution!

Eley said that upon further reflection, she would have kept me on the line and phoned 911 from her home phone to get an ambulance to me. I could have stopped breathing (otherwise known as respiratory distress) at any time, and at least the ambulance would have been equipped with oxygen and trained personnel.

I was so exhausted from the constant twitching and dehydration from sweating so profusely, that my body barely had the strength to recover from that "episode." It took me almost 10 days to recuperate from that hospital visit.

If You Are Still Around …

When I returned to Dr. X after that ICU encounter, I informed her of what had transpired. She really wasn't that alarmed and, in fact, stated that the drugs I was taking, such as OxyContin and Lyrica, were really new. Therefore, there wasn't a lot of data on the interaction between these two drugs, or on any long-term effects. She said she thought I may have missed a dose of my meds. I had enough sense of mind to tell her that they had counted my drugs in the ICU and determined that I hadn't missed a dose. She had no further reply.

The one suggestion Dr. X made was for me was to join a "chronic pain group" to learn how to live with chronic pain. So, being the ever-compliant patient, I found a group that was meeting weekly for 10 sessions, and joined. While I attended the weekly, 2-hour meeting, I met some interesting people and heard some scary stories. While the purpose of the sessions was to clarify what "chronic pain" was, and how to function daily with it, other information stuck with me instead. The majority of the attendees had chronic back issues, while the minority were from work injuries or motor vehicle accidents. Over 85% of us were on OxyContin, and of the 80% that were also taking Lyrica (Pregabalin), over half of us had gained 40 to 50 lbs. Is that not astonishing?? Lyrica was prescribed for nerve pain, and since it was so new, there was little data on it. Although weight gain was one of the side effects listed, it was indicated as being "less likely." Of course, there was no data about it being used with OxyContin. As if chronic back pain isn't bad enough, we all were struggling with how we had gained so much weight so quickly. It was later determined that our metabolism was considerably slowed while ingesting Lyrica, which caused the weight gain. It was a very frustrating side effect.

I continued to see Dr. X for another year, in an attempt to get my pain under control. I still consulted with my family doctor as she was very interested in what was transpiring at the pain clinic. We were both getting concerned with the pattern that was emerging: Each visit ended with more and more OxyContin, longer stretches without follow-up, and my condition worsening. We were both getting very concerned.

During my next visit with Dr. X, she reviewed my meds again, and she added ketamine (a pediatric sedative and also a horse tranquilizer) and clonazepam (a sedative and tranquilizer) to see if my spasms would stop, and to help me function. **AND** she increased my OxyContin by 40 mg AGAIN.

I had mentioned to her that although I had a lot of friends here, my family were all in the Ancaster/Dundas/Hamilton area, about 5½ hours away. Some of my family were questioning why I was still staying in Orleans when I seemed to be getting sicker; they felt they were too far away to help. In addition, some of my dear friends were calling Eley, updating her on how I was feeling and acting. Now I was slurring my words, literally bumping into walls, and barely functioning.

After learning that my family lived so far away, she told me that if I was still around, to come back in 2 months and she'd see how I was feeling. At that point, I felt like she had given up on me. She gave me the impression that I was wasting her time since I was considering moving back home. I told her that I felt that 2 months was too long of a gap, to which she yelled, "Well, you know, I am busy!!" *How DARE she*, I thought! I yelled back, "Well, I'm sick!!" She just looked at me, shrugged her shoulders, and exited the room.

I left that appointment feeling like I had been an inconvenience to her. I felt that she had just thrown more drugs my way without digging further. **It wasn't my fault** that SHE was busy. I didn't deserve to be yelled at. Did she not care about how I would be reacting to this increase? Surely, she KNEW how dangerous these amounts were for my health. How was she going to get me better if she just kept drugging me more? I wasn't someone trying to scam the system or get more drugs. I had a legitimate back issue and I was sick!!! She was supposed to help me!!!! Sorry, if I'm bothering you!!! If she was so busy, she should hire more staff or get another doctor on board to take some of the patient load. With the new medications she had added, and the existing ones that she had increased, I was literally a walking zombie. Maybe she wasn't expecting us zombies to question her!

When I spoke to Eley that evening, she was shocked by the OxyContin increase AGAIN, and the fact that new additional meds were added that were going to sedate me even more. I agreed because I could feel it myself. I was barely able to stay awake when I WAS awake, and I just wanted to sleep. While sleeping was a relief from the pain, the pain I was in while I was awake was still very severe. I had seen this doctor for 10 months and, in that time, my OxyContin prescription more than doubled, from 160 mg per day to 400 mg. And I was prescribed ketamine, up to 4 times per day, clonazepam for night time, and Cesamet (the synthetic marijuana).

I remember thinking, *how the hell did I get here? I am so drugged, I can't even think straight. I can't work, and the specialist doesn't give a rat's butt if she ever sees me again. Now what do I do? I was looking for some direction in getting better, and now I feel more lost than ever. I'm on a train ride to nowhere, and I don't know how to get off.*

Chapter 5

Buying My Ticket to Opioid Hell

I had no idea that when I started attending the pain clinic, my struggles would only intensify. I had prayed to find a doctor who could get my pain under control so that I could return to work and life! I had met people who could explain their pain from injuries sustained in a motor vehicle accident or other accidents, and I called them "the lucky ones." At least they had a diagnosis and a reason why they were in so much pain.

I was still struggling to have the cause of all of my pain identified. But what was so puzzling to me was that the pain was increasing. Was the underlying condition getting worse? Was something bad, like a tumor, growing larger but hadn't been "found" yet?

After each visit with Dr. X, she would increase my OxyContin, usually by an alarming 40 mg each time, and sometimes add another narcotic in the mix. I honestly felt my life fading away. I wasn't getting better but rather worse! Before I visited her, I was able to stay awake for about 10–12 hours a day. But those hours of being conscious were declining rapidly.

I was morphing into a walking zombie. I was slurring my words, when I could find them. I remember a conversation I had with Eley one night. I was trying to tell her that I had just put a glass of ginger ale on the … hang on, what was the word … so we started playing Charades over the phone … "invisible" hand signals. "You know," I tell her, "the thing that is rectangular" …

she guesses a rug … I reply, "No, I put my ginger ale on it. Now Shyna (my cat) is staring into the glass to see what the bubbles are." Eley says, "In the glass?" … "Yes, the bubbles are in the glass, but it's the thing that is flat with the glass top that you put your coffee and tea on." Eley replies, "The coffee table?" "Yes!!!! The coffee table!!!"

I'm no expert, but I'm sure 99% of the English-speaking population would know the word "coffee table." But in my altered state, I just couldn't find it. I KNEW what I was trying to describe, and could find those words, but the "label," the actual NOUN, was elusive.

My enjoyment of reading disappeared. I couldn't even interpret a Readers Digest article … heck, I couldn't even read a paragraph before losing focus. I was constantly rereading the same sentence over and over again but still without comprehending it. It was an impossible activity, so I just quit reading.

Phone numbers were the worst. With all of my doctors' appointments, receptionists were constantly calling to schedule initial consultations or follow-ups. When they would give me the phone number, I just couldn't understand it. It sounded like Greek to me, like someone was mumbling. They had to give me one digit at a time for me to be able to write each one down individually.

But the one thing I missed the most was music. I've always loved music and dancing. My mom used to tell me that I was dancing before I could walk. Music was something that could lift my spirits instantaneously, whether it was pop, rock, country, Latino, or polkas. But the music went away when I got sick. I couldn't handle the additional "noise" that was flowing out of my stereo. It was as if my brain couldn't process separating the lyrics from the music, so each song sounded mumbled and irritating. My soul missed the music the most.

The Addictive OxyContin

Shortly after getting injured and realizing that my pain was still so severe, my family doctor suggested that she was going to increase my OxyContin, from 5 mg three times a day to 10 mg. She informed me that OxyContin could be addictive, but these were very small amounts, which she hoped would be taken for a couple of weeks and that I would recover. I asked her what would happen if I got addicted to it. She said, "We will simply wean you off the drug over a few weeks, and you will be fine." I was comfortable with that information, and agreed with her decision. But after seeing the pain clinic specialist, Dr. X, the anesthesiologist, she kept increasing the drugs after each visit. And still nothing was helping with the pain.

I heard a statistic yesterday that absolutely shocked me. Since the year 2000, over 400,000 people have died from opioids, and over 500,000 babies have been born with opioid addiction. Now, I don't know what percentage of those people and babies are directly related to OxyContin addiction morphing into heroin or crack, but I would suspect the majority. Some patients who were prescribed OxyContin took the required dosage as prescribed, and when the prescription was done, there were no issues. When prescribed in low doses and ingested properly, OxyContin works perfectly. It can be a life saver.

But for others, there are two ways to get addicted to Oxy-Contin: the first is by being prescribed too much of it, and the second way is by ingesting it improperly. OxyContin is a time-released drug, and "contin" stands for continuous release. Some people discovered that if you crush or chew the drug, all of the medication is released immediately, causing the euphoria, the "rush," or the "fix." This is what the addict who chooses this method is chasing after—that "bliss"—but it is short-lived, which only causes the addict to want it even more often.

Personally, I never cut, broke, crushed, chewed, or dissolved any of my drugs, especially OxyContin. But when you are on such high amounts of it, your body NEEDS that drug, just like the addict who is crushing it. I never got "high" from it, but my body was dependent on it, and to deprive it of that chemical compound is referred to as "drug sickness."

OxyContin, since effective when prescribed in small doses and ingested properly, has now been approved for children. My stomach feels sick just typing that statement. With it being highly addictive, I am very concerned that the age of new addicts will become younger and younger, and the negative effects on society greater and greater.

Narcotics vs. Opioids vs. Opiates

I just want to take a moment and clarify a few terms so that their differences are highlighted.

Analgesic

An analgesic is a drug that provides pain relief without causing you to be sleepy, drowsy, or become unconscious. This selectivity is an important distinction between an analgesic and an anesthetic. The most common example is aspirin.

Narcotics

These drugs produce pain relief (analgesia), a state of stupor or sleep (narcosis), and a risk of physical dependence on the drug (addiction). In some people, narcotics can also produce euphoria (a feeling of great elation). While effective at reducing pain, when consumed in high doses, narcotics can CAUSE pain.

Narcotics are further classified under different "schedules" for legal and regulatory categories, based on the potential for abuse and its medical value. This provides the pharmacies and legal agencies with guidelines for storing, recording, research, supply, and access.

Opioids

All synthetic and semi-synthetic (partly synthetic) drugs resulting from opium are opioids. Examples of synthetic opioids are fentanyl and methadone; examples of semi-synthetic opioids include oxycodone and hydrocodone.

All opioids are narcotics, but not all narcotics are opioids.

Opiates – a subclass of opioid

Opiates are those narcotic drugs that are **naturally** present in opium. The four types are heroin, morphine, codeine, and opium.

Based on the descriptions above, I now present you with my prescriptions that I was compliantly taking:

Falling under the narcotics umbrella:

- OxyContin
- Tylenol 3s,
- Percocet
- Oxy IR
- Cesamet

Then there was:

Ketamine – a dissociative anesthetic, which is not physically addictive but can be mentally addictive

Lyrica – an anti-convulsant used for nerve pain

Clonazepam – a benzodiazepine (which can be commonly abused). It was prescribed to me at night time to calm me.

It's no wonder I was sleeping so much! I was so drugged, it's a miracle I didn't go into respiratory distress, stop breathing, and die!

In addition to the variety of opioids available, an increasing number of them can be found right in our own homes, in our own medicine cabinets, and easily accessed by anyone who can open a door.

When I was growing up on the farm, we would often have farm parties. We would boil up our own fresh sweet corn, put straw bales out around the fire pit, and invite our friends for a great feast with some drinks. But do you know what the connotation of a farm party is today?

It's spelled "pharm" party, or a "skittles" party. For those invited, they are encouraged to go into their parents' medicine cabinets, grab whatever pills they can find, and bring them to the host's house, where the pills are poured into a big bowl. Each guest takes a handful of pills with a big glass of whatever liquid they may have, and wait for their body's reaction. Kids are being rushed to emergency rooms, with heart attacks, seizures, and strokes, while others are dying. The ER staff don't even know how to counteract the reactions because the kids don't even know what they've taken; all of the drugs are mixed in the same bowl. A very scary reality.

The Methadone Debate

Let me clarify for you what methadone is.

Methadone, sold as Dolophine and Methadose, is an opioid similar to morphine that is used in treating those with opiate dependence. It is typically administered in a methadone clinic or in a substance use disorder services clinic (SUDS). Methadone is used in a medically assisted drug therapy treatment for those who have a history of opioid dependency, or who want to avoid withdrawal symptoms of illegal drugs, such as heroin. Initially, patients are in a drug treatment program or are required to go to the methadone clinic daily to get their methadone, which provides accountability and structure. After 90 days, the patients may be given a 2-day supply to reduce the clinic visits to three times a week. Methadone can be consumed as a tablet or solution. In some addiction centers, methadone is administered for just 1 year if the patient has not relapsed; however, some patients may require to take it long term.

For some, there is a real debate whether methadone should be used. For those working within drug treatment centers or with addicts, methadone is considered an "opioid replacement medication" for drugs such as heroin. This replacement helps to eliminate the cravings that the addict feels, so that they can focus on the treatment program and getting well. If the addict is being treated as an outpatient, he/she can start to resume their normal activities, such as going to work or properly taking care of their family and children, while checking in daily at their clinic for their methadone. The hope in using methadone is to successfully eliminate the cravings, avoid relapses, and build the confidence for a successful recovery.

However, there is a fine line between a lethal dose of methadone and an ineffective dose. It can be tricky finding the correct dose, and it can have some severe side effects, such as respiratory depression and heart issues. However, it can be effective in blocking the "high" that you get from other opioids, and help in treating addiction.

For those against it, methadone seems to be just a substitute for another opioid, with many similar side effects. As with any drug, it too can be abused and misused, leading to overdoses and death. As well as being physically addictive, the addict can become psychologically addicted to the drug. Some feel that addicts are just trading one drug addiction for another, and delaying the withdrawal process that, if successful, would get them well. Current data shows that 25% of methadone users will stop using methadone after being weaned off the drug over time, 25% will continue to use it, and the 50% remaining will be on and off methadone as they repeatedly go in and out of treatment centers.

Everyday Addicts

When you hear the term "drug addict," what vision pops into your head? Is it a homeless person with long, matted hair, and dirty hands and dirty clothes? Is it a person who is shaking, sweating profusely, and not making eye contact with you, who will ask you for spare change and is a bit scary looking? Yup, that's what my perception was. But let me tell you, that isn't the only perception I have anymore.

With the invention of OxyContin, there has been an absolute explosion of a new kind of addict, one that I have called "the everyday addict." For the majority of us, we aren't hiding under a bridge or walking the streets looking for a fix. We could very well be living next door to you. I have met addicts who got addicted to OxyContin after their family doctor prescribed OxyContin for an ear infection! Yes, an ear infection. And now they are addicted to it while still trying to work full time. We are your neighbours, your friends, and even your co-workers. We aren't getting our drugs illegally off the streets; our drug dealers are doctors. I know that some doctors, like my family doctor, are very diligent about not overprescribing OxyContin; yet there are some doctors who are prescribing OxyContin to their patients, and to others' patients, in exorbitant amounts. Dangerously high levels of this narcotic can kill you.

With OxyContin being so addictive, some people will turn to heroin or other drugs to continue getting their fix after their doctors stop prescribing their Oxy. From what I have read, heroin is cheaper but comes with many more inherent risks. Let's start with the obvious: It's illegal, which brings with it all of the dangerous activity—finding a dealer, meeting the dealer, buying the illicit drugs, and then consuming whatever they claim is the drug. Of course, people have been killed, robbed, or beaten when trying to get the drug, and if they survive that, there is the direct risk of reacting to whatever the drug will do to your system— overdosing is not uncommon. Being caught with the drug will probably lead to a jail term. But for those addicted, the elation of the drug pulsing through their system certainly outweighs the risks involved. Their priority is that fix, period.

Personally, I've never experienced what it was like to be forced to find the drug I was addicted to, find a dealer, find the money to buy it, and then find a safe place to get high. My drug was legally prescribed, legally packaged, and even delivered, with the help of the taxi driver hired by my pharmacy, right to my door. I even called the pharmacy to add my Visa card number to my file so that it was paid for before I even got it. Talk about convenient!!!! But that was the only easy part of this whole adventure. My life was slipping away before my very blurry eyes, and it would become apparent just how much I had lost when my visitors came to town.

Chapter 6

It's Time to Go Home

My friends and family were all getting increasingly worried about me and how ill I was becoming. The back issue was the original problem, but there were so many more issues worrying them.

Rarely, when they called my house, did I answer; it was my answering machine that recorded the information. I was too busy sleeping … A LOT. How could I not be? I was taking so many pills that affected my ability to function that the only thing I could do well was sleep. I was medically sedated, not just tired. There is a HUGE difference. If you've ever had a medical procedure where you have been under general anesthesia or "knocked out" or "put under," you know the feeling. As hard as you try to stay awake, you can't. Your body is metabolizing the drugs that have been pushed into your veins so that you don't remember any of the operation. Now, keep in mind that I was taking these types of drugs on a DAILY basis. This is me, who never even had an aspirin in my house, now consuming these drugs **DAILY FOR YEARS**.

I actually thought I was doing okay when I was awake. I was able to play with my cats and eat something, although it wasn't an elaborate meal by any means. I like to cook, and I think I'm pretty good at it, but it takes a lot of energy, focus, and wherewithal to do it, and I didn't have any of those. So it was usually cereal or a breakfast replacement drink, and soup out of a can and a sandwich. That was about it. My next door neighbour would lovingly pass home-cooked meals on a plate to me, through the side door, and they were delicious and so appreciated. But honestly, I really wasn't that hungry; I was tired. I tried to drink more water when I got up, but that seemed like a chore too.

When my friends did manage to talk to me, they could hear my slurred words, and noted that my sentences didn't always make sense. They could tell by my weak voice that I wasn't well. One of my dear friends, Linda, had told Eley that after a recent conversation with me, she had wondered who she had talked to. Nothing I said made sense, and I didn't even sound like me! When my friends would schedule a time to "pop by" and visit with me, they were shocked at the "Lizzy" that met them at the door. On top of the 50-pound weight gain, I was visibly weak and often had to hang onto the couch or table or wall to steady myself while walking. The visits weren't long either, as listening, and sometimes even talking, was exhausting. They left feeling worse about my condition, and were beginning to question if I should remain living alone in my house.

Finally, Eley decided to come up for the weekend with my best friends and their two children to visit. I still remember being torn about that. I was excited that I would see them, but it sounded like so much work to have visitors, let alone ones that would be **staying with me**. I thought, *What am I going to feed them? What am I going to DO with them? How am I going to keep them entertained? I am so tired and sore.* Of course, they told me not to worry, and that they would bring all the food. Plus, they had some things they wanted to see in Ottawa, so I could sleep while they were playing "tourists." The kids were still quite young, about 4 and 8 years old, so there was always something going on in the Capitol, especially in the heat of summer, in June.

Friday night arrived and so did Eley and my friends. I call them that, but really, these best friends are like family. But still, this was the most activity I had had in my house in months. I had

3 queen-size beds, with a pull-out, double bed/sofa, so I could fit everyone comfortably. Since they had to leave after work that Friday, they didn't arrive until almost 9 p.m. I had slept all day so that I could be awake and (somewhat) alert when they got there. They came with coolers and bags filled with food, and lots of hugs and kisses. That affection was so nice. As they promised, they took care of all the logistics, food prep, activity planning, and clean up. I just had to wake up and be involved. They had wanted me to go out on the bright, sunny Saturday, but I declined. The Cesamet (synthetic marijuana) I was taking made me so sun sensitive that when the sun hit my skin, I felt like I was being burned alive. They enjoyed the Capitol while I slept, and my cats finally had some kids to play with, which tired them out.

But on Sunday, at breakfast, they all looked so concerned. It was very apparent to them that I shouldn't be on my own anymore. They were appalled by the number of pills I was taking and how I was acting. I was walking down the hallway banging into the walls, and they could see how severe my back pain was—I couldn't even put on my shoes unless they were slip-ons. They were afraid I would fall down the stairs when I had to go down to do laundry or sift the kitty litter. But the one thing that surprised them was the amount I was sweating. Small amounts of narcotics can cause sweating, but with the amount I was on, that side effect was amplified. A couple of times that weekend, Eley asked me, "Did you just take a shower?" to which I replied, "Nope, this is how I sweat!" I would be absolutely and completely drenched. And then I would get cold and feel sicker.

The Decision Is Made

Standing in front of me, Eley finally said, speaking on behalf of my best friends and other family members, "We've decided that you need to come home. Enough is enough. You can't stay here by yourself; it's just not safe. If you fall, who would find you?

You're just too sick." After spending the last 30 hours with me, they had seen enough. And for me, it was as if the decision had been made for me. For months, I had heard my friends' and family members' concerns about me staying in Orleans, but I honestly thought I would get better and that all would be fine. I had to admit that I finally agreed with them. I couldn't find an answer up here, and I needed help just to function. Even in my sickened state, I could see how worried they were, and their words were crystal clear. I needed to come home!

I told them that I already had an appointment on Tuesday with my family doctor, so I would tell her then that I was going home. I would have to list and sell my house, pack up my stuff, and move home, but it was time. I felt it in my core. I didn't know how it was all going to happen in my physical state, but it just had to. My life depended on it.

I met with my family doctor that Tuesday. I told her that with Eley and my loved ones' guidance, I needed to go home. I told her that Eley and my friends felt it wasn't safe for me to be living on my own anymore, and she agreed. My family doctor and I had gone to high school together and she knew Eley and my best friends, and she knew they had my best interests at heart. After my appointment, I got into Pablo's car for the ride home. He asked me, "How was your appointment?" And I replied, "I'm going back home." He looked at me and said, "I think that's the right decision." Out of all of my friends, Pablo and Gemma saw me the most, and they knew how very sick I was.

When I got back to my house, I sat down on my couch and started praying. I wanted to be home as fast as possible, so I told God that. I gave him a real deadline though: I wanted to be home by the end of this month, July. It was July 8th. I called my real estate agent, Sheila, who had helped me find this house—my very first house—and told her I was moving back home. She was excited for me and said that she would get the paperwork going and list my house. The first step was initiated.

They say God works in mysterious ways, and He answers your prayers. I can attest to that. Within 5 days, my house was sold for full asking price, with a closing date of July 31st. I had hired movers to pack up the entire contents of my house, and my belongings would arrive at my new address on August 2nd. Since being in a car for at least 5½ hours was out of the question, I had booked a flight for August 1st. But I had to get my cats home, so Eley had offered to drive up and bring them home for me. To add icing to this cake, Eley had found us the perfect house together, in Brantford, with a move in date of—you guessed it—July 31st, so that we could live together and she could take care of me. I couldn't believe how easily things fell into place to get me home. I guess God felt I needed to get home quickly too! God is good!

Moving In With Eley

I am so grateful to have such a wonderful sister, Eley, and to say we are close is an understatement. We are identical twins within a set of triplets, and we have never, EVER had a fight. No, really!!! We feel it would be like having a fight with yourself. Now, I know what you are thinking: *That's impossible!* But as God is my witness, that is the truth. We finish each other's sentences and are very linked mentally. We can't read each other's minds per se, but we do "feel" things between the two of us.

In high school, unbeknownst to me, Eley had sprained her left ankle in gym class and had gone home. At about 11:15 a.m., my left ankle had started to throb horribly, but I couldn't figure out why. I hadn't twisted it or anything, but man, did it ever ache. When I got home that afternoon, I told my mom, "My ankle is killing me!" She replied, "Go see your sister; she's on the couch." Sure enough, I go into the living room and there's Eley with her left ankle all bandaged up. I lifted my left leg onto the couch and asked her, while pointing at my ankle, "Does your ankle hurt right here?" She said, "Yup," and then my pain went away. No lie! I'm just glad neither of us ever had kids ... and shared that pain event!

Some people, like our closest friends, don't think we look anything alike, and others have never been able to tell us apart. Consequently, our favourite day was always April Fool's Day, April 1. For those of you who are unfamiliar with this tradition, the morning of April 1st, until noon, is the time to play a fun prank on someone or tell someone a white lie.

Eley and I would ALWAYS switch classes in high school during second period, which started at 11:30 a.m. We would have to tell each other where to sit because the other one was literally going into a new classroom, full of people we knew but not knowing where our desk was! Switching could be a little nerve racking because each of us was going into a new classroom, listening in on a subject we weren't taking! But at most, we only had about 25 minutes until we would announce our April Fool's joke and return to our real class.

In Grade 13 (that tells you how old I am, because there WAS a grade 13 back then), Eley and I were taking the same chemistry class and had the same GREAT teacher, Mr. Esposito. He had a great sense of humour, so we knew that this April Fool's Day would be fabulous!!! The day finally arrived, and we shared the information about where to sit (it's those little things you need to know!). So, I headed to Eley's social studies class, not having a clue of what THAT was about, while Eley headed into my chemistry class, being right up to date with the course! Little did I know, Eley's class was to discuss the chapter they were supposed to have read the night before! I thought, *this is going to be the longest 25 minutes of my life!* It was! The teacher asked me a question, and I had not a clue what to answer, so I just said, "I don't know." That surprised her, so she asked someone else. I just kept looking at my watch. Finally, 11:55 a.m. arrived!!! I asked to go to the washroom and left the classroom. I then purposefully walked to Mr. Esposito's room and knocked on the door. He answered and I asked, "Can I talk to Eley?" He looked at me confused, and said, "I have Lizzy in my class," and I replied, "No, you don't." The class erupted in laughter because NO ONE knew we had switched. The next day, when I went into his class at my regular time, he asked me, "So, who do I have in my class today?" The prank worked well.

Since we get along beautifully, I felt blessed that we would be sharing a home together. I needed the help. Eley had found us a beautiful 3-bedroom bungalow with a finished basement, an enclosed back yard for our cats, and a hot tub. It was right around the corner from her current home, so we decided that we would bring my two cats and her cat into the house at the same time. That way, we figured, it would be new territory for all 3, and they could figure out the pecking order. Little did we know that it would take the cats 9 MONTHS to tolerate each other!!

Eley works at a local hospital in Hamilton. She also taught medical terminology at Mohawk College part time. While she doesn't work with patients directly, she is actively involved in the data, funding, and how the hospital functions. She is very a caring, giving person, and is the best "nurse-ka" (my Polish slang) I could have ever had. After moving in, Eley decided to get a security system installed; not for fear of someone breaking in but for the security that I could push one button and have help, such as police, fire, or an ambulance show up. That gave her some comfort.

Eley recognized quite quickly the pattern that was now my life. I was sleeping 22 hours a day. Eley would leave for work and come home after 10 hours, and NOTHING in the house would have moved, including me! There were no dirty dishes in the sink, and no signs of activity either. I hadn't gotten up since she left for work. After she would make us supper, she would wake me up so that we could eat together, and we would watch TV for about an hour. Then I would crawl back into bed. I only got up to take my medications, which were contained in 15 different bottles. She was so worried. Little did she know that she would be my legal caregiver for 3½ years, keeping me alive while working full time.

Two days after I moved in with Eley, I got a call from one of my dear friends in Ottawa. She told me that Pablo had died that morning of lung cancer. I knew he had been battling it for 2 years, but he still drove me to my appointments, did my errands, and brought me food. He often commented that he felt no pain and was shocked at the amount of pain I was having. He was such a dear friend and, honestly, I wept after hanging up the phone. As sick as I was, I booked a flight back to Ottawa to attend his funeral on August 9th. His wife, Gemma, was as involved in caring for me as Pablo was, and I needed her to know what an impact he had made on my life.

New Contacts

Before leaving Orleans, I had searched and luckily found a new family doctor in Hamilton, which was about a 35-minute drive from our new home. I felt grateful that I had found a family doctor so quickly in my area, as we had quite a family doctor shortage in Ontario. On September 15th, Eley drove me to my first appointment with Dr. Smith, and we both went into the examination room together. I needed Eley to "translate" what the doctor was going to tell me, and give her a brief history of how I ended up here.

I can still recall the look of horror on her face when I presented her with my list of medications. She looked up from the paper and asked me, "You take all of these daily?" to which I replied, "Yes, I do." "Wow, I'm surprised you physically made it in here." I told her that my family doctor and I had agreed together to stop seeing the pain specialist, as we didn't think her approach of increasing the narcotics was working. In fact, we had talked about decreasing the OxyContin before I moved back home, but then I left within the month. Dr. Smith agreed that my liver and kidneys wouldn't be able to handle all of the stress of all these drugs for much longer. She made a note to test me every 3 months in order to carefully review my liver and kidney health. Eley told her that my back pain was the original complaint that had led to us being there in her office. She then ordered a new MRI and CAT scan for me, so that she could begin to investigate my case herself. She refilled my prescriptions for me, hoping that the new tests would guide her to a better treatment plan. She told me that she would begin weaning me off the drugs once she got the test results back.

A few days later, Eley and I went into our new pharmacy for the first time to pick up my prescriptions, including the one for OxyContin. I introduced myself to the pharmacist, and after he checked my identification, he looked at me and said, "You're Elizabeth?" I said, "Yes." He replied, "I can't believe you walked in here. You are taking enough narcotics to tranquilize an elephant!" He told me that he had called my doctor about my Oxy-Contin prescription after seeing a daily amount of 400 mg, because he thought she had made a mistake. The pharmacist said," I thought she should have written 40 mg per day, but she had put down 400 mg. But she told me, "I wish it were only 40 mg. It's 400 mg." Now, if your pharmacist is shocked at narcotic usage, what does that tell you?

While we were hopeful that Dr. Smith would be able to help me, Eley felt she needed to find me a specialist to deal with my back issues. Eley and I had never had to deal with something like this before. We had been healthy and had no experience with narcotics; so, for Eley, seeing me like this was like holding a helpless baby in her arms, begging for help. She saw how sick I really was, now that we were living under the same roof, and knew that my body couldn't handle this assault for much longer. There are no retirement parties for addicts or those who ingest excessive amounts of drugs—they just don't live that long!

One of Eley's friends, who had been in several car accidents and had suffered some horrible injuries, gave her the name of a specialist, Dr. Eileen Groves, in Burlington. She told Eley that

Dr. Groves was known to work on the severest of cases with great success. Eley finally felt, for the first time, that there was some hope.

We met with both my family doctor, Dr. Smith, and Dr. Groves, to discuss my dire situation. After informing both of them that we wanted them to help me at the same time, Dr. Groves came up with a treatment plan for weaning me off the pills, which Dr. Smith completely agreed with. Then Dr. Groves got to work on trying to mend my injured back.

The Pile of Paperwork

Every night, when Eley would get home from work, she would bring in the mail, as I was still unable to walk the short distance to the mailbox without getting a back spasm. There seemed to be a never-ending pile of paperwork to be completed—insurance forms, reimbursement forms for treatments received, long-term disability paperwork—and then there were the official government forms. Eley would always help me with all of them, as they can be confusing to complete even when your mind is sharp, but with a blurry, drug-filled brain, they are almost impossible.

I'm not sure if you have ever been on sick leave, but the amount of paperwork you have to complete is incredible. Doctor's notes to prove you are still sick are constantly being demanded from every source: insurance companies, my own employer, and the government. I realize that they are trying to prevent fraudulent claims from people who are pretending to be sick, but unfortunately, the truly sick patients are the ones that have to suffer through this paperwork nightmare!

I had applied for Canada Pension Plan disability benefits because I was truly disabled. What a journey that one was. With mounds of papers, test results, doctor's letters and forms, it was a very stressful experience. And then, initially, it was denied. I cried when I got that letter. Here I was, sicker than a dog, drugged to the hilt, barely able to walk because of back pain, and they were saying I wasn't sick enough. Really? Then Eley read the entire decision, which gives you the option to appeal. And we did. And won. But what a pain in the royal behind that fiasco was.

By this time, it was June of 2009, and I had been off work for over 4 years. Due to a backlog in my own employer's human resources department, they were extremely delayed in following up with my sick leave schedule. But then, they got caught up. Since I was feeling a bit better since starting to decrease the meds, one of my daily chores was to get the mail. It forced me to get outside and go for a quick walk to start building up my stamina and strength. Eley made me promise that I would carry my cell phone with me in case I needed help. When I got to the mailbox that day, I was surprised to find a huge envelope from my work. I carried it back to the house and proceeded to open it at the kitchen counter. At this point in my life, I still struggled to read and retain information, but I could get the gist of the first page.

Due to my lengthy absence from work, my employer needed to know my status and if/when I was returning to work. I understood that they had to figure out what to do with my position, as it was being temporarily filled in my absence. So they were giving me 4 options: return to work full time, with doctor's approval; quit; retire with medical grounds; or if I chose none of the above, I would be dismissed.

Then the additional 60 pages—**yes, 60 pages!!!!!**—detailed the various options of my decision: if I would get to buy back part of my pension, severance pay, and monthly pension amounts, based on what I decided, et cetera, et cetera. What???

You know those rare instances in life when you hear tragic news—for example, of someone dying, like Princess Diana or John Lennon—and you know EXACTLY where you were when you heard the news? Well, this was one of those instances for me. I know exactly where I was in the kitchen when I read this letter. Initially, I was shocked. Then I was hurt. Why didn't some-one just call me to let me know that this was the next step? And then I was frustrated because I couldn't UNDERSTAND all of it. How was I supposed to READ and COMPREHEND all of this and make a reasonable decision?

I called Eley, bawling. I managed to mumble out some words that she could piece together. I told her about the letter, and she calmed me down by saying that we would look at it together when she got home. She wanted me to just leave it on the counter and relax. We would figure it out together. She made me feel better, like always. And we did figure it out. I retired with medical grounds, retroactive to the ripe old age of 42. But if that paperwork was the worst shock I had to endure, it was nothing compared to the withdrawal hell awaiting me.

Chapter 7

Welcome to Hell

Withdrawal Hell

If anyone tells you that withdrawal is easy, they've either never gone through it themselves or they are just straight out lying to your face. I can honestly tell you that it is the worst thing I have personally experienced. I wouldn't wish it on anyone.

If you check "Dr. Google" for the common symptoms of withdrawal, you will find quite an exhaustive list:

- Anxiety
- Goosebumps
- Restlessness
- Insomnia
- Yawning
- Runny nose
- Watery eyes
- Dilated pupils
- Body aches
- Sweating
- Vomiting
- Belly cramps
- Diarrhea
- Fever

- Shaking
- Fast heartbeat
- Rapid breathing
- High blood pressure
- Hallucinations
- Seizures

If you are addicted to drugs, your withdrawal, including how many symptoms you experience from the list above, and the severity of them, is unique to you. Your withdrawal will depend on how long you had been taking the drug(s), the dosage consumed daily, how healthy you are, and how you are quitting the drug (medically supervised withdrawal, "cold turkey," or substituting another drug for it).

Before I was prescribed all of these drugs, I just didn't understand why addicts would relapse time and time again. If they had already made up their minds to stop taking drugs, why would they start using again? Just to get high? Maybe, but I think the real answer is this: The extreme body pain and sickness they feel is just too much to handle. They just want the pain to end. After personally suffering through withdrawal symptoms, I can honestly say that I get why they relapse.

Initially, withdrawal is like having the worst flu you've ever had, multiplied by 1000. Every cell in your body is **screaming** for the one thing you are trying NOT to give it: the opioid or narcotic, which in my case was OxyContin. Although I never experienced getting "high" from OxyContin, it was obvious that my body was physically dependent on it, which is part of addiction. When your body perceives that the amount of OxyContin in your system is lacking, it feels like it signals every cell to go on high alert and beg for the drug.

As the day begins to wind down, Eley and I are watching TV and just enjoying some time together. It's nice to be awake when she's home. But as *Jeopardy* begins, I start getting that really sick feeling deep down in my stomach and bowels. *Oh crap, it's starting again,* I think to myself. It's like clockwork. At 7:30 p.m., every night since I started weaning off the drugs, I go through an hour of sheer hell, which Eley and I have nicknamed, my "Power Hour." For some unknown reason, an hour before I am supposed to take my nightly drugs, my body begins to revolt against me. And it isn't playing nice.

Now, I don't want to gross anyone out, but the next few paragraphs are pretty explicit, with some gross details. I apologize in advance.

I get up off the recliner and "rush" to the bathroom as fast as my aching back can allow. I know I'm going to be in there a while; I always am at this time of the night. By now, Eley knows what to expect. She enters the bathroom shortly after me, but she comes with supplies: a fresh wash cloth, a hand towel, and a big glass of cold water. She knows what is about to happen, and it won't be pretty. She finds me already sitting on the toilet with my underwear around my ankles, and my head inches away from the bucket I am holding on my lap. I never know what will happen or what end (head or butt) will be affected, but I know I am in for a rough ride, again.

Oh, boy, I feel so nauseated. You know when you keep swallowing because it will hopefully keep whatever wants to come up, down. Well, that's what I keep doing, over and over again. My lips are so dry, but even though I keep licking them, it doesn't help. They just won't retain any moisture. I keep exhaling through my mouth. God, I feel sick. Oh, here we go. I start heaving with a force that is coming, I swear, from the very tips of my toes. I retch and retch until I finally vomit. I think to myself, *oh, at least I hit the bucket this time.* I keep retching while Eley steadies the bucket. She grabs the face cloth, runs it under cold water, wrings it out, and gives it to me. *No, wait, here I go again.* I throw up for 4 solid minutes, with a force that is hurting my stomach. *Where is all of this liquid coming from? Oh …* I get a breather and lean my head back a bit. I wipe my mouth off with the face cloth. It feels so good because it is so cold. I feel so hot.

Eley asks, "Are you okay?" I answer, "I'm not sure yet." Then the nausea starts again, but the force of it surprises me. I barely have time to aim for the bucket when this projectile vomit is violently expelled out of my mouth. Some of it gets in the bucket... "Oh, God, now I have to clean that up," I say to myself. But Eley says, "Don't worry; when you are done, I'll take care of it." My poor Eley, what I have put her through. And she never complains, never says, "Clean it up yourself"—nothing. She is an angel. While the heaving stops, Eley empties out the bucket, washes it, and gives it back to me. She knows we aren't anywhere near done yet. Then she cleans up the floor and the wall. All I can do is sit on the toilet and wait.

Now my bowels are making me feel so awful, I clench my stomach and cry. *Oh, not this too!* While the vomiting has stopped, for now, my bowels have decided to join in on the fun. With a wicked cramp, my bowels empty violently, and it just keeps coming and coming. I don't even get up off the toilet; I just push the handle down to flush while I'm still sitting on it, because I know I may not have enough time—no, not even the 5 seconds it takes to stand up, flush the toilet, and sit back down again— before the cramps hit again. And again, and again. I am so weak that I feel I can barely sit up on my own on the toilet. Thank God, our bathroom vanity is literally a finger's length away from me. I put my left forearm on the vanity counter, and my head collapses against it. Now I'm sweating and my entire body is aching.

I can't believe it. *What the hell is going on?* My legs start to shake, just like little wiggles at first, but then it's like I'm driving over a washing board—but I'm not in a car; I'm still on the toilet. The shaking gets so bad that I have to push my knees together. Remember those vibrations that I couldn't tolerate? Yup, my body is vibrating from the shaking, and my back begins to spasm. I'm trying to hold my legs together and grab my back at the same time, but I don't have enough hands. Eley kneels down quickly and holds my legs together while I writhe in pain from the spasms. And then, just as fast as it started, the shaking ends.

While my back is calming down, Eley says, "Breathe. Breathe." I don't realize it, but I've been holding my breath during this whole shake-rattle-and-roll episode. I take a deep breath, and then another one. *God, please help me.* I feel so sick and weak, and now I'm drenched in sweat. Eley says, lovingly, holding some mouthwash in front of me, "Gargle this." *Oh, she thinks of everything.* I gargle and spit it out in the bucket. Then, with a glass of water in front of me, she says, "Drink this." *Yes,* I think, *I will.* I am so thirsty; I feel like I've been on a raft in the middle of an ocean, for weeks without water. I drink the entire 2 cups all in one shot. Eley fills the glass again and leans against the vanity. She has such concern and fear in her eyes, and it is etched on her forehead.

While I try to gain my strength, I put the bucket on the counter. Eley takes it and washes it out again. Then I put my elbows on my knees and hold my head in my hands. I am burning up. Eley leaves the room and comes back holding a fresh t-shirt. "Here, give me the one you are wearing." I look down at my shirt. I didn't have a chance to notice before this, but my t-shirt is drenched in sweat and other particles of stuff I don't want to mention so I take it off eagerly. The fresh t-shirt feels refreshing but I'm boiling. I clean myself up while I have this "break" from bodily functions.

I say to Eley, "I don't think I can sit on the toilet much longer. My back is killing me." With a short pause, I ask her, "Can you help me down on the floor?" Without hesitating, she gingerly helps me get on my knees and I lean over to sit down on my butt. "Where's the bucket?" She had it in her hand before I even asked the question. So here I am, with an excruciatingly painful back, lying on our cold ceramic bathroom floor and loving it. While it isn't cushy, it is deliciously cold. Eley gives me a fresh, wet, cold facecloth that I drape over my forehead. With the bucket near my head just in case, I lie there for about 5 minutes.

How can this happen day after day? The level of sickness I feel within my body is hard to quantify. It's like every cell is screaming, yelling, and protesting, with placards: "Give us drugs; give us the drugs," because the drugs aren't coming in as fast as usual. There are no other thoughts in my head except for, *Give us the drugs. God, I feel so sick. Just shoot me already!!! It can't hurt as much as this.* At times, I'm honestly thinking, *I'm just going to take those extra OxyContin pills, and all this sickness will stop.* But wait. What? *No, don't do that,* I remind myself, *you'll have to go through all of this again!! You're going to make the withdrawal process last even longer!!!* Then I come to my senses and keep praying that this hour is almost up. No, I was NOT going to give in and take the extra OxyContin. I can't go backwards and go through this hell again!

I'm sure that Eley, who was witnessing this frightening scenario nightly, wanted to say, "Just take a pill; we can start again tomorrow," but she never did. I didn't want to have to repeat any of these "Power Hours" again. With the nausea, vomiting, sweats, body shakes, and diarrhea, during those early evening hours, I spent a lot of time in my bathroom. But once 8:30 p.m. arrived, I would take my nightly drugs, and all of these symptoms would gradually disappear. Eventually, the "Power Hours" weren't as violent, and then weren't lasting as long. My body was beginning to heal.

Now maybe it's easier to understand why addicts relapse when they are withdrawing from narcotics. I've had norovirus previously, but this "Power Hour" and withdrawal were so much worse than that. I just wanted the sickness from the withdrawal to end. And I was under the doctor's supervision during all of this. I can't even begin to imagine the sickness that addicts who are incarcerated experience, alone, in a cold cell, forced to go "cold turkey" without a doctor's supervision. Or those who can't afford rehab or find a doctor, and are trying to withdraw on their own. It's a miracle that more of them don't die from it. Honestly. I know that a lot of people believe that the addict "did this to themselves," and they somehow "deserve to go through withdrawal" without any help. Treatment centers will often offer a medical withdrawal process where the addict will be medically supervised, and often medically sedated, while withdrawing for the first few days. But for those who are trying to kick the drugs on their own, I truly have newfound respect and much empathy for them. They have chosen an extremely hard and lonely battle.

When my family doctor began to help me with reducing the narcotics dosage, some drugs I just stopped taking immediately, like ketamine and Tylenol 3s. But certain drugs, like OxyContin, can't be stopped "cold turkey," because it could kill you, especially with the dosage I was on. When I started, I was ingesting 400 mg of OxyContin a day, which is an astronomical amount. Most doctors start patients on 5 mg or 10mg, and may go up to 40 mg if the pain is severe. I was on **10 times** that amount **EACH AND EVERY DAY!** Crazy, isn't it? Under my doctors' direction, I began reducing my OxyContin by 5 mg every two weeks. Doesn't sound like a big deal, does it? I mean, 5 mg is nothing, right? Most weeks, it wasn't noticeable, but there were those weeks where my body just felt like it was impossible. During those really difficult weeks, my doctor would tell me to keep at the same dosage for 4 weeks instead of 2 weeks, and then, if I was okay, we would continue decreasing the Oxy by 5 mg, two weeks later.

ICU Visit #2

On a clear morning, in November 2010, I had to drive to Hamilton for a hearing test. Since we only had one car at this point, Eley and I drove to Hamilton together. My doctor had given me the all-clear to drive again, as I had decreased enough of my narcotics to be safe on the road. So I drove Eley to her work, and then I went to my hearing test. While my back was sore, driving was manageable.

Since I only had a couple of hours to wait until I could pick up Eley, it didn't make sense to drive back home, only to have to turn around and drive back in. I had arranged to drop in and visit with my cousin, Krystyna, and her husband, Steve. We've always been close, and I was looking forward to seeing them. After a nice lunch, my back was starting to really ache, so I crawled into their bed for an hour before I had to leave. After thanking them for their hospitality, I drove off to get Eley.

Once I picked up Eley, she got into the driver's seat for our ride home, and she said I looked tired. I was feeling a little tired, but otherwise, I felt okay. About 10 minutes later, while we were on the highway and going about 110 km (65 miles) per hour, I suddenly felt really hot, so I lowered my passenger side window. Eley told me that she could turn up the air conditioning, so I closed the window. But I was still so hot. I kept shifting in my seat and couldn't get comfortable. Eley kept looking at me with confusion in her eyes. I rearranged the vent outputs so that all of the vents were blowing on me.

While Eley was driving on the 403, I decided to recline my seat and CRAWL INTO THE BACK SEAT of her Nissan Altima! To me, it didn't seem like a strange thing to do, but of course, Eley couldn't figure out what the heck I was doing. You have to remember that I could barely walk without pain, let alone crawl over seats and contort myself to get into a back seat! Once I got into the back seat, I lay across it with my head behind the driver's seat. But that wasn't comfortable. So, I sat up and then pro-ceeded to lie down the other way, with my head behind the pas-senger's seat. I did **this 3 more times**. Eley was yelling at me, "What are you doing?" I replied, "I'm trying to get cool." I finally found a spot and stayed there for the rest of the drive.

When we got home, Eley grabbed a cold glass of water, sat me down in the kitchen, and told me, "Drink this." It was exactly what I needed; it cooled me down, for about 10 seconds. I asked Eley, "Can you get me another glass?" As she was refilling the glass, I went to sit on the recliner in the living room. She gave me the glass of water and I drank it all. I asked her, "Can I get another one?" Off to the kitchen she went again. But when she turned around to return, she couldn't see me in the living room. She found me in my bedroom. "I have to get these sheets off my bed; they're too hot," I cried, while pulling at the sheets. I stripped the entire bed. She said, "Just lie down and try to relax." I stretched out on the bed and tried to follow her directions. Or so I thought.

The next thing I remember, I was STANDING ON MY BED, moving like some contortionist from Cirque de Soleil, trying to get these imaginary bugs off of me. Eley couldn't believe her eyes. Then I jumped—yes, jumped—off the bed and went into the living room. I sat on the recliner, exhausted. By this time, Eley had seen enough. Not many people have their specialist's home phone number for emergency purposes, but we did, and she used it. She called Dr. Eileen.

Eley told Dr. Eileen, with panic in her voice, "Eileen, Lizzy is acting really weird, and keeps screaming that she has all these 'bugs' on her." Eileen asked, "Is she breathing?" Eley was stunned. "What? Yes, she's breathing!!" she replied. Eileen then replied, "It sounds like a drug reaction or withdrawal. Is it time for her to take her medications?" Eley knew my schedule, and said, "She still has about half an hour." So Eileen replied, "Give her the dosage now. That should calm her down within the next 20 minutes or so. If it doesn't, call me back. Go give her the pills."

Now, that sounded easy enough, but Eley couldn't FIND ME! She went into my bedroom; I wasn't there. She checked her bedroom; I wasn't there. She checked the bathroom and living room; nope. I wasn't on the main level. So downstairs she went, even though no lights had been turned on; the downstairs was pitch dark. She turned on the lights and then started searching for me. She finally found me, sitting on the toilet in the windowless bathroom, in the dark. I said, "Hi!!" with real surprise in my voice, like I hadn't seen her for weeks. Eley asked me, "What meds do you need to take now?" And I told her what I needed, without missing a beat. Eley ran up the stairs to get the meds, and remembered that we had a list of my meds on the fridge. She double checked the list of meds with the info I had given her, and was surprised that I was right. As she was getting my pills in the kitchen, on the main level, I walked past her, heading down the hall, slouched over in pain, on route to my bedroom. She followed me into my bedroom and watched me take my meds. Then I had to lie down on my bare mattress. I was melting. I wanted to get up, but Eley told me to just stay there and rest.

Eley went back into the kitchen and, within 2 minutes, she came running into my bedroom. I was screaming at the top of my lungs and swearing like a sailor. Now, for anyone who knows me, they know that I rarely swear. While I know all the swear words, I can usually find other words to express myself. But now it felt like there were thousands of bugs crawling all over my body, and swear words were the only words coming out of my mouth. And not just the "minor" swear words but the ones that would make a trucker blush. I was using these words repeatedly while screaming and contorting. At this point, Eley could barely get me to sit down, so she called in extra help: Julia, our best friend.

Julia lives around the corner, literally, so Eley gave her a quick call and she was at our place in a flash. When Julia came in the front door, she could hear my screams and my swearing from my bedroom, and she looked at Eley with shock in her eyes. She followed Eley to my bedroom and watched in amazement as I was standing on my bed trying to get the bugs off of my arms … and then off of my legs … and then off my back and then out of my hair. Julia said to Eley, "I didn't think she could move like that with her back pain." Eley replied, "She can't on a 'normal' day."

But this was no normal day. This was my second full blown drug reaction. I didn't have the twitching in my shoulder like the first time, but now I was completely consumed with getting these imaginary bugs off of me. They were everywhere: in my ears, in my nose, and in my mouth, and there were thousands of them. I didn't see them, but I didn't have to—I **FELT** them. No sooner would I "remove" them from my arms, then they would be on the backs of my legs or down my thighs or somewhere else. They were so annoying that I didn't even know Julia was in the room until she grabbed my arm. *Oh, Julia's here,* I thought, and I kept reacting to the bugs. She told me, "Lizbit, why don't you sit down on the bed," and I nonchalantly said, "Oh, okay." I sat beside her and tried to explain about the bugs while still contorting!!!!

The phone rang; it was Dr. Eileen checking up on me. Eley told her, "Lizzy is still contorting and screaming about the bugs!" "Then you need to call an ambulance now." Eley hung up and called 911. While they told me that the ambulance was on its way, Eley and Julia walked me to the living room to wait there. I replied, "I hope the ambulance guys are cute!" I still laugh at that reply. For one split second, I wasn't worried about the bugs!

The ambulance seemed to get there quickly, and I tried to tell the paramedics what was happening, in between Eley's comments. We always had a list of my medications, with the daily dosages, hanging on the front of the fridge, in case of emergencies just like this one. Eley gave them my meds and that list. Then they started asking me questions. "Elizabeth, do you know what day it is?" *Oh, that's easy,* I thought. "Wednesday." Then question number 2: "Do you know what year it is?" "2008." *Right again,* I thought. "What city are you in?" *That's easy.* "Orleans," I replied. The imaginary buzzer went off over my head. The paramedics looked at Eley, knowing that we were all in Brantford. They had heard enough. I agreed to get on the stretcher while they guided me. They buckled me tightly and lifted me and the stretcher inside the ambulance. I don't remember a lot during the 10-minute ride to the hospital, but I do remember them asking me more questions. I have no idea how well I answered those ones.

When we arrived at the hospital, the doctor met me with a couple of nurses. While the EMTs gave their report, those lovely nurses were trying to get me comfortable and calm. It was difficult to react to all of the bugs while being buckled in, but once they removed those restrictions, I started flailing again. I was so agitated, and I begged them to make the bugs stop! The doctor reviewed the list of medications, and said, "I have never, in 22 years of being an emergency room doctor, seen ANYONE on as many drugs as you. These are deadly." He was appalled. I replied, "I'm weaning off of them, so these aren't as strong now." He replied, "You are damn lucky to be alive!!" I didn't feel so lucky at that moment, that's for sure. Then I saw Eley beside the stretcher, and she gave the doctor the update on my situation; and yes, all of the drugs, she assured him, were prescribed in much higher doses by a pain specialist. He was alarmed, shocked, and disgusted at the same time. "This shouldn't be allowed. How can a doctor, a pain specialist yet, with a conscience, think that prescribing these are okay?" We didn't have an answer.

He gave me some clonazepam, which he said was a tranquilizer that would stop the "heebeegeebees." I loved that official name. Within a couple of minutes, the nurse came over and said, "Elizabeth, we are going to have to move you out to the hallway. There's been a terrible motor vehicle accident, and we will be getting 3 severely injured patients any minute. Don't worry, we know you are still here."

While Eley and I stayed in the hallway, the nurse came out to get some blood work. Within an hour, I was starting to get really tired as the clonazepam had successfully "killed all the bugs." So I told Eley, "Please go home. You don't need to wait here for me. I'll get them to call you when I can go home." I knew that the doctor and nurses were completely overwhelmed with the severity of the crash victims. My results would have to wait.

About 12 hours later, I was woken up by the doctor, who was standing beside my stretcher that was still in the hallway. He wanted to discuss my test results, which included the blood work and the urine sample I had provided. Urine sample? What urine sample? "I don't remember giving a urine sample," I told him, but he confirmed that indeed I had. Now, as a female, giving a urine sample is much more complicated. It requires balance and a lot more precision than if I were a male. But, as much as I searched my memory, I couldn't find any trace of that experience. Eley told me later that, yup, I had given them a urine sample. In fact, she had even helped me walk to the washroom in my socks (I had left my shoes at home), and then helped me balance while I filled the sample container. Strange, I didn't remember that!

The doctor told me that this episode was probably a drug reaction from all the pills I was taking. Unfortunately, he wasn't really sure when or if it would happen again. But he confirmed that if I kept taking all these drugs, it was bound to happen eventually. I told him I had been weaning off the drugs for the last 3 months, and I planned to keep going until I was completely off of them. He wished me luck.

On the drive home with Eley, she had to piece together the events of the previous 15 hours. I had a very foggy recollection of those hours, even though they just happened. I didn't remember going downstairs in the dark or sitting on the toilet while I gave Eley a rundown of what I was taking. I don't remember Julia being there, other than when she asked me to sit on the bed. I sure as heck don't remember giving a urine sample at the hospital, which is the most alarming omission. But Eley assured me that I did. I was told by my doctor that because my body was under such stress, the brain had to determine what the list of priorities was as it went into a self-protection mode. Keep me breathing was priority #1; making sure I remembered the details was priority #999. I was okay with that. The recovery after this episode was 8 days of rest.

A couple of years after I had stopped the OxyContin, my specialist confided in me that she really didn't think I would ever get completely off of it (the OxyContin). She thought, with that high of a dose, it would be impossible. I'm really glad that she didn't tell me that. I'm happy to say that I proved her wrong and have been narcotic free since July 1, 2011. Being Canadian, July 1st is Canada's birthday, and a special day for me on a personal note. It was a horrendous journey, filled with a lot of sickness, hurt, pain, disappointments, frustration, and tears—but I did it!!

I have never had a craving for OxyContin since, nor have I ever relapsed. I just don't crave it. But I also never got high from it either. I took just the amount prescribed by my doctor, and I never crushed it, chewed it, injected it, or smoked it. I had gradually built up a huge tolerance to it, and I know that it made me really sleepy, but that was it. I never had to find extra pills of "Roxy" "on the street," or get OxyContin prescriptions from several doctors to fuel that need of getting "high." I consider myself very lucky that I was allowed to wean off the drug slowly. Shortly after I was "clean," a new form of OxyContin was produced, called OxyNEO, which was impossible to crush, so that it couldn't be abused by addicts.

I know I'm one of the "lucky" ones. Most addicts never get off of the OxyContin, and some will substitute a cheaper, illegal drug, such as heroin, once their doctor refuses to refill their prescription. As with any illegal drug, it may lead addicts to go to places and do things that they would have never done before to get the drug, had they been clean. The risks and dangers of that lifestyle are unfortunately well known.

Chapter 8

And So the Recovery Begins

While searching for a doctor to help me throughout this struggle, I certainly came across a couple of really shady ones. Of course, from LOOKING at them, you can't tell that. It's only after you give them a lot of your hard-earned money, and precious time, that you realize you aren't getting any better; they are just getting richer. I had that awful experience with a chiropractor in Orleans, who claimed to be a born-again Christian to boot. He suggested a treatment plan that involved me going for an adjustment 4 times a week for 3 months. And man, did he ever have a booming business. I kept seeing the same people in the waiting room each week. But magically, NONE of us were getting better!! We all were tricked into thinking that we needed him. He said my back was so "bad" and I was so hypersensitive that he wanted to start with just adjusting my neck. But he never got to my back. Week after week, he refused to adjust any part of my back, so I cancelled the rest of my appointments. What a con artist.

When I started my treatments with Dr. Eileen, I knew that she was an extraordinary doctor with almost magical abilities. One of Dr. Eileen's specialties is craniosacral therapy (CST), a form of bodywork or alternative therapy using gentle touch. She will start the session by cradling my head to palpate the synarthrodial joints of my head. She then continues to touch my back, hips, or pelvic bones. The therapy works by regulating the flow of the cerebrospinal fluid and keeping your energy moving. While some people don't believe alternative therapies are helpful, I am a big fan of CST. It seems to release blockages, or get more oxygen flowing or something, but it works wonders for me. And the bonus is, it doesn't hurt—not one iota.

A Unique Therapy Visit

Dr. Eileen also had a chiropractor on staff, Dr. Dwayne Frood, if one of her patients also needed a chiropractic adjustment. She told me that a consult with him would be beneficial. After meeting with Dr. Frood ("Call me Dwayne," he said), he told me that adjusting my neck, like the last chiropractor did in Orleans, wasn't going to help. He needed to adjust my back, and particularly the area around my right sacroiliac (SI) joint, between my lower back and hip. I thought, *Oh, Lordy, here we go again.* But I trusted Dr. Eileen, so I was willing to give this chiropractor a chance. I didn't think my back could cause me more pain, but boy, was I wrong.

When Dr. Dwayne told me that he had to adjust my SI joint, I stared at him in disbelief and absolute fear. He explained that even if he started from the neck down, everything would get out of alignment because the SI joint was the one that was out of whack. So after processing how this would help me, and praying for courage, I agreed to let him adjust me.

Now, you have to understand, I didn't let ANYONE touch my back unless it was absolutely necessary. I mean, **I couldn't even touch MY OWN back** half the time! If someone was walking behind me, my right arm automatically swung behind my back and stayed at my waist, as my shield of protection, in case someone accidentally got too close and bumped into me. Now I was contemplating letting a chiropractor crack my back. I took a deep breath and asked, "Are you absolutely sure you NEED to do this?" He nodded his head up and down, and said, "Yes, I'm sure." *Damn,* I thought. I had hoped he would cave in under my questioning, but he didn't … "Okay, go ahead." He warned me that he would crack me at the count of three, and honestly, I was secretly hoping he would never get past 2 … but he did. He cracked me and I screamed, and then I proceeded to cry, in a fetal position, for 5 solid minutes while Eileen held my head in her hands and Eley rubbed my hands. Then I got one of the worse headaches of my life!! And if that wasn't enough, I went into shock where my teeth were chattering loudly and I became horribly cold. Eileen massaged my head and neck to help with the pain, while Dwayne hooked me up to an IFC (interferential current) machine and a laser machine. It took me 2 hours to have enough strength to go home, and another 6 days before I felt half normal again. After about a week, I actually felt like I was moving better, ever so slightly. Yes, there was hope!!!

Dwayne and other chiropractors in Dr. Eileen's practice have been able to adjust me, and what a difference that has made. Dwayne felt that the landscaping incident that I had while removing the cedar bushes, was the main cause of my back pain, which was also in my upper and middle back, and right hip. Dr. Eileen told me that there was also a great deal of soft tissue damage in my back and right hip. She explained that when sedated patients are in the hospital, the nurses regularly roll them to prevent bed sores and soft tissue damage, from sleeping in the same position all the time. Unfortunately, I wasn't in the hospital when I was sedated, so I had slept the majority of time on my right side, in the same comfortable position. Consequently, my right hip, sacroiliac joint, and thigh had all suffered major soft tissue damage.

All of my adjustments basically had the same pattern as above but with less severity over time. Sometimes I didn't cry for more than 30 seconds, but I always got a headache. Eley said that although it was very painful for me, it was fascinating to watch from a medical perspective. Each appointment lasted a minimum of 2 1/2 hours.

The **worst** adjustment to date was when Dwayne had to

crack me in 3 places—he normally did only one or two adjustments per visit. I braced myself for all 3 adjustments, but I didn't see this coming. After the crying and the headache, I laid on my left side while Eley and Dwayne put a big foam pillow between my knees and covered me in blankets. Within about 5 minutes, I couldn't move my arms or legs. I was scared and amazed all at the same time. I kept telling my arms to move, but they wouldn't. Dwayne and Eileen stayed in the room with me until I felt my limbs again, and then, of course, didn't I have to go to the bathroom. What timing!! It took both Dwayne and Eley about 5 minutes to get me the 50 feet down the hallway to the bathroom. Eley helped me in the bathroom, and then it took another 5 minutes to get me back in the examination room. After about 2 hours, I finally told Eley that I thought I could go home now. I think she had visions of us both sleeping there overnight. So, Dwayne and Eley held me up as I walked to the car. Eley already had the car warmed up, with a blanket and pillow waiting for me in the front seat. While we were driving home, I told Eley that she would need to get someone to help me into the house.

When we got to our street, Eley drove straight to our friend's place, who lived just a few houses from us. She banged on the door, and when Rick opened the door, Eley told him that she really needed his help getting me in the house. Rick didn't think twice; he grabbed his jacket and hopped in our back seat. I told Eley not to drive into the driveway because the bumps would be too much for me to handle. When we got to the bottom of the driveway, she opened the door for me, and she managed to get my feet on the ground before I just started bawling. It took me another 2 minutes before I had the strength to stand up. With Rick holding my left arm, and Eley holding my right, we started walking up the driveway. It felt like I had to get to the other side of a football field, but in reality, it was only about 60 feet. It was like I was in a daze. My head was swimming, my body aching and weak, and all I kept repeating to myself was "left foot, right foot, left foot, right foot," while Rick and Eley kept me upright.

"Wait, wait," I cried out. "I need to stop." So there the three of us stood, in the middle of the driveway, while I tried to find the strength to keep walking forward. I had to stop, but I eventually got to the front door. Eley opened the door, and once I stepped inside the house, I leaned against the wall and cried for 2 minutes solid—this was so hard, and I was so exhausted. Rick and Eley held me up while we walked to my bedroom, where I collapsed on the bed. I'm not sure how long I cried before I fell asleep. I was really ill after that adjustment, but luckily, the temporary paralysis only happened once. I'm still not sure why I reacted so violently during my treatments, but eventually, the severity of the reactions lessened and then eventually disappeared.

Ginger Baths

With the number of narcotics and other drugs that I had been ingesting for years, my specialist knew that my body had absorbed a lot of toxins. And she was right. When I slept, I would sweat like crazy, and the crap that came out of my pores at night was right there on my pillow case each morning: dark brown spots. Lord knows what the stuff was, but the body only has certain methods of excreting the nasty stuff: through your bladder, bowels, mouth, nose, or pores. Normally, a person is moving throughout the day, expending energy, showering, and all of the other normal functions we take for granted. But because I was so ill, I was only awake for about 2 hours a day, and with my movement being almost non-existent, sweating was one activity I could do while I slept. What a multi-tasking chick I am, eh? Thinking back, I did do a lot of laundry—my bedding, pillowcases, and night shirts!

But the sweating wasn't just when I was sleeping. Hyperhidrosis (excessive sweating) is quite a common side effect of narcotics, and I was the poster child. When I moved in with Eley, she would ask me, "Did you just take a shower?" and I would reply, "Nope, that's just me sweating!" I would be drenched in sweat from head to toe, and would have to change my clothing often throughout the day.

Another way I expelled toxins was by taking baths using a "ginger bath recipe" that Dr. Eileen had shared with me. She told me that similar recipes had been used in Chinese medicine, aboriginal medicine, and East Indian Ayurvedic methods. It's quite a simple recipe but very effective at reducing my pain.

The first time I tried this recipe, Eley prepared the bath with all the ingredients for me. She then had to help me into the tub as I was really struggling to go from standing to sitting normally, and it was darn right impossible within the tight confines of a tub. She gave me a hand towel that I would dip in the water and lay on the front of my body while I was lying in the tub, so that I would keep as warm as possible. After the 20 minutes, she helped me get out of the tub, wiped off my feet, and helped me to get into bed. I kid you not, within the first 2 minutes of being under the covers, my pain level had gone from a 9 to a 3—what relief! But the most amazing part was the amount I was sweating!

With this recipe, the toxics are being pulled out of your system while the magnesium in the Epsom salts are being infused. Magnesium helps prevent muscles from cramping, and that was exactly what I needed. I would take a "ginger bath" twice a week, and found it to be one of the best remedies I have ever discovered! For a copy of the ginger bath recipe, please go to my website: AJourneyIntoOpioidHellandBack.com.

One morning, after a very long night, I awoke feeling horrific. I mean, just nasty. My head was throbbing, my brain was foggy, and I just felt terrible. When I came into the kitchen, Eley took one look at me and said, "You look awful!" I replied, "I feel awful." With a look of desperation of her face, she said, "Why don't you drink something, like a big glass of water?" I thought to myself, *well, it couldn't hurt*, so I followed her advice. Within 5 minutes, it was like someone had flipped a switch. My headache had eased, and I didn't feel quite as sick as before. She deduced, "You are dehydrated. No wonder you feel so awful when you wake up. With the amount you sweat, and the amount you sleep, you aren't drinking enough; your body is chronically dehydrated." Now it's no surprise that with all my sweating, my body was being depleted of not only dangerous toxins but also much needed salt, other minerals, and of course, water.

And to make matters worse, I was malnourished too. Dr. Eileen suggested a supplement to help me get the essentials back into my body, as I wasn't awake long enough to consume the proper nutrients. It helped immensely. I was beginning to feel stronger and less dope sick too.

Do You Have Anything to Declare?

When I first moved back home to live with Eley, I was truly at my sickest. I was barely functioning, and my only daily goal was to **just keep breathing**, literally. After a grueling year of recovery, and Eley taking care of me, we decided we both needed a vacation.

Eley and I had booked a 10-day cruise to the Panama Canal, on Royal Caribbean's ship, Jewel of the Seas. Eley felt that going on a cruise would provide both of us with a beautiful distraction during my illness. Since there would be a doctor and nurse on board, I would have access to 24-hour medical care if needed. Plus, I could always go back to our cabin when I needed to lie down.

Since we were flying out of Buffalo, New York, we decided to drive to the airport and leave our car there for the duration of the cruise. Being that we lived in Canada, we had to cross the international border between the U.S. and Canada, at the Peace Bridge in Buffalo. Before we left, I had received a 2-week supply of my drugs, from my pharmacist. I was weaning off the drugs, so they had put an elastic band around the pill bottles for the first week of meds, and for the second week, since the dosages were different. My doctor had given me a detailed letter indicating what pills I was taking, with the corresponding dosages.

I had decided, on that early January morning, that I would be much more comfortable in the back seat of the car for the 90-minute drive to the border. I had a blanket and small pillow, so I was fairly cozy while Eley drove. I had placed all of my pills in my carry-on duffle bag in the trunk. I didn't try to hide them because I knew that I had the doctor's letter to prove that they were all legally obtained and all mine.

When we approached the border, Eley pulled up beside the booth and rolled down both her window and mine in the back. The border patrol asked for our citizenship, and we replied, "Canadian." He then looked at me, all covered up in the back seat, and asked Eley to pop the trunk. She complied. The duffle bag with my drug "stash" was the first bag on top of the large pieces of luggage. We could hear him unzipping the bag. *Sure enough,* I thought, *he's found my pills.* He must think he just hit the jackpot for illegal drug smuggling. The border patrol officer then came along side of the car, with his hands full of my pill bottles, and asked, "Who is Elizabeth?" I replied, "I am." He asked, "So, what's with all the drugs?" In my head, my thoughts were, *he probably thinks these are divided into separate orders to be dropped off to different people.* With my slurred speech, I started to explain what I was going through, and pulled out the doctor's letter. He asked to see it and read it while we waited. He gave me back the letter and asked, "Do you have any alcohol or cigarettes that you're taking into the country?" And we replied no. "I'm going to put these back in the bag." Once he did that, he closed the trunk and then proceeded to let us go through. We were relieved to say the least. I guess my decision to be in the back seat was a little odd to him.

Little did I know on that trip that I would discover one of the best pain relievers: salt water. I had been taking Epsom salt baths regularly, and I knew that they were helping. But when I got into the luxurious salt water pool on the ship, it was my piece of heaven on Earth. It was magical. My pain was reduced to the point where I could actually float and get relief from the spasms and cramping. On the 5th day, we took a 4-hour excursion to a beach, and I stayed in the water for 3½ hours. It was so wonderful to feel "normal" again. I had previously stopped taking the medication Cesamet, which was causing my sun sensitivity, so to feel the sun on my skin was healing. Eley helped me balance while walking on the beach to get into the ocean, and I didn't want to get out. I knew that there was a "blanket of pain" waiting for me on that shore, and it would envelope me for the entire time until I could get into the ocean again.

Battling Depression

Depression has a lot of stigma attached to it, but luckily, we are seeing some positive steps in bringing this disease "into the light," by having people admit to having it, and dealing with it. In Canada, we have the "Bell Let's Talk" initiative, which is helping people talk about having depression, and therefore slowly reducing the stigma.

For years, our culture has been very accepting of seeking medical advice when an affliction happens below the neck line. If you break your arm, you go to your doctor for help. No one doubts that you have a broken arm, and they certainly wouldn't condemn you for seeing a doctor or taking time off work until you are better. Unfortunately, for mental health issues that occur—those above the neckline—this usually isn't the case. It is only recently that there is a slow change happening for those afflicted with mental health issues; and personally, it's about time. Depression is a chemical imbalance in the brain, plain and simple. It is no different than having your thyroid functioning poorly or your sugars out of balance. In each of these cases, we have medications and treatment plans to get you feeling well again, and to help your body get back to functioning correctly.

I admit that having to deal with chronic back pain, I sometimes deal with depression. When I was withdrawing from all of those drugs and would hit a really bad week, my best friend, Julia, would be so good at trying to lift my spirits. She would say, "Lizbit, remember just how far you've come. Look at what you can do now; you couldn't do those things before!" I had to agree with her. And it did make me feel better. But it is still difficult being in constant pain, and it's really depressing to not be able to do things I once did easily. This isn't just an aging issue; this is a mobility and stamina issue. I have to think twice before I bend or try to twist (still a no-no). Pacing myself at tasks is still hard, and I often overdo it and end up in bed for days. At times, I feel like the world keeps spinning but I'm no longer allowed on the ride. It stinks.

I find that I have become much more introverted than ever before. I was a real social butterfly before "all this" happened. Now, I admit that sometimes, I would rather stay at home than go out … anywhere. When I'm blue, it feels like such an effort to be sociable, to engage in conversations, and to be extroverted. Just getting showered, dressed, and getting somewhere is a chore, and I tire so much more easily now. There is, from time to time, that thought that is playing over and over in my mind, screaming, *Why bother?*

I have to convince myself that I **will feel better** after seeing my friends and family, because I love them, and **I truly want to be with them**. I really do. I push myself to go out, to be helpful to others, to volunteer, to do errands, and drop by for a visit. But there is still a small dark part of me that keeps reminding me that *it's going to take a lot of energy, you're going to be more tired, your back is going to be sore, and why don't you just stay home?*

Before I got sick, I also had things to talk about. I was working, playing sports, travelling, and I had hobbies, so there were always things going on and things to talk about. But when you are sick, especially for YEARS, those topics that you always talked about may not exist anymore. I can't work anymore, I can't play sports, and I have limited hobbies. Consequently, I don't have much to talk about. Luckily, I still travel to all-inclusive resorts, and I take cruises because, then, my hotel room is within reach. I can't backpack or take those long bus tours through Europe because I can't lie down when I need to. Therefore, trekking to see Machu Picchu, in Peru, has definitely been removed from my bucket list.

To add to the cruelty of this entire situation, one of the drugs I was prescribed caused me (and millions of others) to gain massive amounts of weight—50 pounds to be exact! The medication essentially screwed up my metabolism. I mean, let's be honest, I was only awake for 2 hours a day, and I wasn't eating a lot as it was. It was baffling to me that I had gained so much weight during that time. Not only is the extra weight causing more pressure on my back, and is dangerous for my overall health, it is devastating on an emotional level. As if I didn't feel sick enough, I now had to deal with the weight issue, which makes me feel even worse. I couldn't find a cause for my back pain, I couldn't find relief from the pain, and now, I had ballooned to over 215 pounds. I think any reasonable person would be depressed. While I've managed to lose about 30 pounds, my struggle to lose the excess weight still continues.

There is a definite difference between the Lizzy before all this happened and the Lizzy that you see today. Suffering from depression, for me, is a lonely battle, but I'm grateful that it doesn't strike me often. I try not to let others know that I am depressed. When I am around those I love, I am usually happy because I'm able to be sociable. I don't let my family or friends see me when I'm really sick, because I don't like to burden others with my health problems. Therefore, they rarely see me depressed or in a lot of pain, because I will just stay home when I'm feeling like that. In my case, my absence is what speaks volumes.

But while my recovery was difficult, this opioid crisis is costing all of us, even if you aren't the addict. But what's the real cost?

Chapter 9

Being Sick Isn't Cheap

Cost to Me Personally

Where do I even start? I can't even begin to calculate what this experience has cost me. If I calculate the cost in a financial way, let's start with the drugs, shall we?

I certainly kept my pharmacy busy. They were filling all of my prescriptions while my savings were being drained. Just my Oxy-Contin and Lyrica prescriptions alone cost me $1200 a month. Now, luckily, my drug plan covered 80%, but that still meant I was paying $240 a month for those 2 alone; not to mention the other 13 drugs I had. If I did not have a drug plan, I would have been paying an additional $2000 a month for all of the drugs I was on. Plus, there were vitamins, supplements, ointments like Biofreeze (a topical cream that I LOVE and buy in vats), back braces, neck pillows, and body pillows, which were all paid for by me. Oh, I still to this day have the walker I got when my back spasms make it difficult to walk, and unfortunately, at times, I still have to use it.

On top of that, I had physiotherapy and chiropractic coverage for $300 each per year. At $40 a visit, that coverage was gobbled up quickly. I was going 3 times a week to physio, for 14 months, and chiro three times a week for 4 months, just in Orleans, not to mention when I moved home, so those were added expenses. Then there are those treatments and modalities that just aren't covered: prolotherapy, Botox, craniosacral treatments, parking costs (so that my friends who drove me didn't have to pay), taxis, et cetera, et cetera. Geez, I haven't even begun to calculate the cost of the care I received from Eley. How do you put a dollar amount on that? A caregiver would have been required to help me bathe, do my laundry, make my meals, purchase my food, and then let's not forget those lovely "Power Hours," plus the cleanup after those. Then let's calculate that cost for 3½ years—yikes!!! Thank God, I DIDN'T have to pay for that yet!

Now let's talk about the cost to my career; yup, let's just kiss that one goodbye. With a snap of your fingers, your goals in life have been destroyed. Everything you planned has been ripped from you. If I calculate the possible career advancement, lost wages when I was getting Employment Insurance (which is only at 55% instead of my normal salary), loss of pension because I stopped working so early, and having to buy back years of service (in my case, $25,000 worth), that was a huge, huge hit. Plus, I missed out on the challenge of a new position, and the pride that I would have had in doing my best in a new job.

Let's just dabble in the mental stress part, shall we? I went from being independent to being totally dependent, on not only the drugs but on others. I needed help with EVERYTHING: doing groceries, going to appointments, understanding medical terms, doing errands. Oh, and let's just for the record, say a few words about the paperwork when you're sick. If you weren't sick before, let me tell ya, you will have a massive headache when you have to go through the mounds of forms, doctor's notes, appeals, and Lord knows what else, like I did. It is exhausting, frustrating, and most of it, so unnecessary. This paperwork is lengthy, repetitive, and confusing as all get out. For some reason, most insurance companies believe that doctors got their degrees off the back of a Cheerios box, and ask for more and more doctor's notes, or they have to get their "specialists" to review them. They hold up benefits unnecessarily, or they just stop them whenever they want. I was already sick before I started filling out the paperwork, but now I was convinced they were trying to give me a heartache.

And then, when I was about 2½ years into my recovery, I finally could read again and comprehend the words. What a blessing that was!!! I felt it was time to write a letter to the College of Physicians and Surgeons to have them investigate what I (and many others) felt was the overprescribing of narcotics to me by Dr. X. I thought, *she could have KILLED ME!* And what if I didn't have Eley, my family, or friends, who watched out for me and took care of me! If I hadn't had that support system, I would have been dead for sure. I didn't want one other person to have to go through what I did. So I wrote a lengthy official complaint.

A couple of weeks later, I received a call from a representative of the College of Physicians and Surgeons. She asked me, "Why did it take you so long to lodge your complaint?" I told her, "Why? Because it has taken me almost 3 years to wean off of the drugs she had prescribed, and I've only recently regained my cognitive ability." That was the absolute truth. She asked me a few more questions and then ended the conversation. A few weeks later, I received the reply. The final decision: Dr. X wasn't negligent in my care, but they felt she might benefit from some training on weaning a patient off of drugs. WHAT????? ARE THEY SERIOUS??? They thought the drugs I was given were reasonable!!! I still can't wrap my head around that. If you have pharmacists, doctors, emergency doctors, paramedics, and others, shocked and commenting how anyone can possibly function on the drugs you were prescribed by ONE doctor, how is it that the College didn't see that too??? It still infuriates me to this day.

Now, let's just mention a bit of the emotional aspect; it has been devastating. I went from being a self-sufficient, independent, travel-ready, life-loving, contributing member of society, to a sedated, completely dependent, "requiring a care-giver" individual. The cost of that loss of independence and health is immeasurable. I lost **YEARS** of my life—**YEARS!!!!** I slept them away because I was so sedated, and when I was awake, I was in agony. I couldn't go to any festivals, concerts, or dances; I couldn't play cards with all my Newfoundland friends until 3 a.m. in the morning anymore; I couldn't go see a movie or go out for dinner with my friends; I couldn't invite my friends over for a homemade Polish meal anymore. I was a prisoner in my own body because of the greed associated with OxyContin. People were making too much money off of it and all the others, by producing, selling, and prescribing OxyContin, period!

But I ask you, what would you be willing to spend to get your health back? I honestly tried to find a way back: back to the Lizzy I recognized, back to the life I recognized, and back to being with my family, friends, and coworkers. I tried EVERYTHING I could to get better, but the drugs counteracted that. In fact, taking the drugs hurt my health immensely, not just in the short term but in the long term. My back issues are chronic now, and I do believe that was because I was sleeping so much in the same position. Lord only knows what the long-term effects on my organs could be from consuming all of those pills. Time will tell.

Cost to Society

When I was really sick, I was actually able to provide a bit of extra "economic employment" to a few people in my area. Specifically, I had to hire a maid and a lawn service crew, but that was the only positive thing I did for society.

The drug epidemic is taking a major toll on our society. Employed individuals are becoming addicted and are now unemployed or even unemployable. For those who are business owners, it equates to the loss of not only their business revenues and taxes, but also to the loss of their employees' jobs. And then there is the ripple effect: If people aren't going to work, there is loss of revenue for transit systems, day care centers, and then additional costs to replace that individual and rebuild their work force. For those who had jobs with benefits, those coverages are now stopped. With the additional financial burdens, many rely on social services such as welfare, food banks, and shelters. Our social services are stretched to the limits.

Children are going into foster care because their parent(s) can no longer take care of them because of their addiction. If the children are older, they may be forced to care for younger siblings, without proper guidance or skills. Or worse, they could be left to fend for themselves and perhaps on the streets.

Hospitals are being stretched to the limit with addicts presenting with overdoses, drug reactions, gunshot wounds from illegal drug activity, motor vehicle accidents from impaired driving, and the list continues. Addiction centers are at capacity, leaving many unable to get the proper treatment or guidance they need to get clean.

After the addict can no longer receive their OxyContin legally, they are forced to find it illegally, which brings an entire new set of risks to the addict and society. Obtaining illegal drugs, I hear, is a risky hobby, especially if you don't have an income coming in. Thefts of narcotics from your local pharmacy are quite common; in fact, the Orleans pharmacy I shopped at was robbed for narcotics, twice, while I was living in the city. People are being robbed, stabbed, shot, and killed trying to buy or sell drugs. Crime increases, and it risks the lives of innocent bystanders, first responders, and all those in the area.

Let me be clear here. The people I'm calling addicts are those who once were contributing members of society: business owners, employees, stay-at-home moms and dads, your friends, your family members, and your neighbours. These drugs are so addictive and so prevalent that this opioid epidemic is second only to the COVID-19 pandemic we are currently experiencing.

It's incredible to me that we have all become increasingly numb to not only the statistics but the real meaning behind them. For example, 30 years ago, school shootings were unheard of. When the first one happened, people were in disbelief. How could someone target innocent children and their staff? How could someone target a "safe haven," where there are no security guards or weapons to protect it, only to use a lethal weapon to try to destroy the innocent?

I believe it's the exact same situation with the narcotics overdoses. The narcotic pushers are targeting the innocent while knowing full well what the destructive "weapon" can do: It destroys lives. Does it matter who was shot or who overdosed? I think some people would have a great deal more sympathy for a school child than a "drug addict," but it doesn't make either situation any better. In both situations, there is so much unnecessary pain that is created, whether you are the victim, the family, one of their friends, or society as a whole.

What incredible things could these people have contributed to the lives around them or society if they had survived, or even better, not been targeted in the first place? What would the children have become? What new inventions or contributions could they have been allowed to discover or offer? What if the addict had never been prescribed the highly addictive narcotic? What contributions could they have made? What businesses could they have run, or employees could they have hired? What about the beauty and kindness that was buried with them that never got to be expressed?

Now, when yet another school shooting makes the news, we barely flinch. And unfortunately, when we hear the weekly narcotic overdoses, it's just another statistic. It is so sad.

Cost to My Family and Friends

It is true that an addict's journey can be expensive for their family and friends, depending on what type of support they are providing. The cheapest form of support, but the most valuable, is love. I know it sounds cheesy, but knowing that my loved ones had my back (no pun intended) and were supporting me was priceless.

If you want to be specific and get right down to the nitty gritty, my family and friends did pay for certain things like gas and parking costs when they took me to appointments, even though I offered to pay for it. Some were buying me food or bringing me over delicious meals they had lovingly prepared.

For others, the costs are greater. If their addicted love one no longer has an income and/or benefits, their friends or family members may offer their home as a safe place to stay. While I agree that some addicts may not make the best roommates, there are many that can be; they just can't afford an expensive addiction rehabilitation treatment centre. If you don't have savings, a home equity loan, or insurance coverage that pays for the treatment, friends or family members may be willing to pay for your stay at one of these treatment centres, but do your homework as they are not created equal. Some are very professional and offer wonderful services, including counselling (one-on-one, and groups) in a well maintained "residence," with nutritious food and professional help available 24/7. Others are no better than a poorly run youth hostel, with too many people to a room, poor food options, no counselling, and even fewer rules and restrictions. Buyer beware.

But the real cost to family and friends—those things that really take their toll on them—are in the things that you can't truly measure: stress, worry, and frustration.

I can't even begin to measure how much stress Eley was under during all of this. Before I moved back home to live with her, she was calling me twice a day just to make sure I was still alive, literally. I was getting sicker every day, and while I was living alone in my home, she was beginning to question how much longer I could stay there on my own. My friends were so worried as well, and some were calling Eley as little informants, updating her on how sick I was. Eley had witnessed some of the torturous procedures I endured, but it wasn't what I wanted her to see; it really upset her. When we moved in together, I know she was not sleeping well. She kept checking on me during the night to make sure I was still breathing. Here she was, working full time at a demanding job while taking care of me, for years. I often say to her that she got the worst of it. At least I was drugged too much to know better, but she was lucid throughout all of it.

My friends and family didn't know what to do either. They kept telling me to come home because they were worried about me being "alone all the way up there," and I'm sure the feeling of helplessness was really hard on them. I could see the look on their faces when I would join them at their homes, when I would be sweating profusely and looking pale. I can't even count how many times I had to lie down while their parties continued downstairs. Or even when I had to leave much earlier than I usually did after a family gathering, or the numerous times I declined their invitations. The worrying they did about me took a toll on them too.

So here's what you can expect if you are a friend or family member trying to help your loved one, the addict.

Chapter 10

The Rollercoaster Ride for Family and Friends

What They Can Expect

Okay, I'm talking to you: the friend, the family member, or the caregiver. This is an illness, a sickness, and an addiction, to which you may never have been witness, and its boundaries seem to have no end. It's like being on a rollercoaster ride that never stops. Sometimes you are chugging up a super steep hill, not knowing if you are going to make it to the top; other times, you are enjoying the view, and then sometimes you are screaming down a slope way too fast, not knowing where you will stop. It is a path that, if you are living with your addicted loved one, you will be walking too, but more so from the sidelines.

When your addicted loved one is really sick, they may hide away from you, because they aren't feeling sociable and don't want to around family or friends. I know, when I was severely ill, there were a few times when severe back spasms hit without warning, and I couldn't hide before they were witnessed by someone other than just Eley. One particular incident happened at my hairdresser, Jennifer's, when I was about 2 years into my recovery.

We have known Jennifer since we worked together in the summer of '85, and she remains a dear friend. I knew Eley and I had our hair appointments at 5 p.m. that day, so I made sure I had a really good 3-hour nap in the afternoon. I had to ensure I could handle the drive there and back, plus the time it took for a haircut and colour for both of us. Jennifer knew how sick I was, and tried to make the appointment as quick as possible. She even kept a package of frozen peas for me to put on my back when it got really sore.

While she was drying Eley's hair, I went to use the washroom in her shop. Since I had time to kill, and we were the last appointments of the night, I thought I would help her clean up by emptying the garbage from the washroom. I bent down to grab the waste basket and, when I came up, I screamed one of the loudest screams ever. My back was spasming. Now, I was only about 10 feet away from Jennifer and Eley, literally around the corner, so I managed to balance against the door frame and inch my way to a chair just behind Eley. Eley leapt up and helped me into the chair. I was clutching my back, screaming while it kept spasming. I don't know what it's like to be tased, but from what I've seen on TV, I was contorting and screaming the same way as someone who was being tased. The spasms were so severe that I would scream out after each one hit. I was in so much pain, and I couldn't get them to stop. Then I just started crying. I honestly don't know who was crying more, me or Jennifer. While she had heard me explain what the back spasms were like, this was the first time she had SEEN them, and by the look on her face, she was terrified! And so was I. Every time I tried to move my legs, it was like a hot branding iron was being shoved up both sides of my spine. I told Eley, "You've got to take me to the hospital." She replied, "Okay, let's go."

Eley and Jennifer helped me walk ever so gently to the car while the spasms continued. Eley opened the car door, and I looked at the seat and thought, *how the hell am I going to get down there?* The car seat in her Nissan Altima looked like it was 20 feet below me. I knew that going from standing to a sitting position was going to be hell, but I had no other option. They helped me gingerly sit on the side of the seat for about 2 minutes in order to catch my breath, because the worst, I knew, was yet to come. I now had to maneuver my legs and body to slide into the bucket seat. Now, I know most of you have never had to consider this, but let me tell you, after having back issues, bucket seats are really hard to get into. It's just the design of them, with that little dip in the middle, while the sides sort of go up to hug your legs … yeah, that's not good. For me, it was almost like another level change, and moving across the seat rocked my pelvis side to side, which sent more spasms up my spine. After finally getting into the seat, I collapsed into it, bawling. And all that was just to get me into the car! Now that isn't what I wanted my friend to see, but unfortunately, she was the unsuspecting witness. Poor thing.

If you are in close contact with your loved one going through recovery, you are going to witness those withdrawal symptoms that I listed at the beginning of Chapter 7, but I honestly can't speculate to what degree. You will probably see the pain, the agony, and the sickness firsthand, and it won't be pretty. It can be soul crushing to watch. Like I mentioned before, each person is unique, and their experiences are their own.

You are going to have to be a bit more tolerant, because your loved one may not be feeling well enough to join you in social outings or family gatherings. They may have to leave early. But please keep inviting them. They need to feel included, just like before, even though they may not show up as often. They really are trying to join in, but their illness is preventing them from doing so. You are going to feel hopeless, frustrated, and feel like you don't know how to help. That's okay. Just keep supporting your loved one.

You may have to fill out the paperwork, and do the driving, errands, and all the rest, but that won't last forever. Now that I am so much better, Eley and I laugh that I have become her personal assistant. I can do errands, shopping, and all that fun stuff, because I can drive again!!!! I have my independence back, and being in a car, alone, going only where I want to go, is freeing!

Patient Advocates

I think the biggest role that you (family, friends, and care-givers) will have is that of patient advocate. You have to stand up and fight for your loved one, the addicted one. I wasn't the only one prescribed OxyContin who got addicted; there are **MIL-LIONS** of us. You have to find help for us, because when we want to start the journey to become drug free, we are too sick to understand how.

How do you even begin to tackle the labyrinth that we know as our current healthcare system? I know that I am blessed to live in Canada, with the amazing health care available to all Canadians, but it can be so confusing, as I'm sure it is in other countries as well! My logical processing of information was null and void with all of the meds I was taking. When I moved in with Eley, she came with me to every doctor's appointment. I needed her there because I just couldn't comprehend what the doctor was saying. Heck, I couldn't even stay awake. Looking back, I should have had someone with me when I went to my Dr. X appointments at the pain clinic. They could have recognized the pattern of increasing the drugs, and begun to question it! But hindsight is twenty-twenty.

Where Do You Even Begin to Get Help?

Unless you enter a rehab program, there is little if any guidance out there to help you along. You are going to have to search to find a doctor, specialist, or treatment centre that can help your loved one regain their health and their life. I know that it sounds daunting, and it can be, but you have to be diligent and determined. If your loved one can't afford rehab, you are going to have to search for a doctor who can help them wean off the drug(s) in a safe way; there is no rushing this process. It is a long and winding road (hey, that sounds like a song … oops, focus, Lizzy, focus), but it is worth the ride. If you don't like one doctor's opinion, go find another one. You have a RIGHT to a second opinion—use it!

Be willing to try other forms of therapy, even if it sounds "hokey-pokey" or New Age, or whatever you want to call it. If your loved one has some other health issue (and they probably do because that's the pain that caused them to go to the doctor's office in the first place to get the OxyContin), try the conventional therapies like chiropractic care, massage therapy, acupuncture, and the like. If those don't work, try what are called the "non-traditional treatments." These can also be interpreted as "probably not covered by your insurance company" treatments; you may have to pay for them, but they could be the answer you are searching for. I had never heard of prolotherapy, intermuscular stimulation, or a micro-current treatment (like a TENS machine), but I tried them. Some of them didn't work, but at least I tried them. Others have been essential to my ongoing health, like chiropractic care and massage therapy, which I still get regularly.

But the craniosacral treatments by specialist, Dr. Eileen, was the treatment that saved my life. Her amazing healing abilities and skill in diagnosing severe health issues saved my life, and I can't thank her enough. It was a very difficult treatment for me to endure, but it may not be as painful for you. It worked to reverse all of the years of drug abuse and dis-ease in my body. Laser therapy was also used during each visit, and I am a firm believer that it heals painlessly. I truly believe, with every cell of my body, that without craniosacral and laser therapy, I wouldn't be the person I am today. I would either be in a nursing home right now, drooling into a bib, or in my grave. I am a much healthier person because of these "newer" modalities.

You are going to get stressed, and so will your addicted loved one. Please be gentle with yourself. Do something healthy to rid yourself of the stress—take your dog for a walk, hug your cat, have a nice long bath—whatever it takes. It's hard on everyone, so be good to yourself.

For those full-time caregivers, make it a priority to get yourself some respite care. At least twice a month, get away for a night or two to relax and restore YOURSELF. Going through withdrawal and recovery will be hard on you as well, so it's imperative that YOU get to sit back and get a breather.

For those looking in from the sidelines, running errands or sending over a freshly made meal, or even picking up a drive-through meal is always appreciated. There is a big burden here, and any little part you can do will certainly ease the load. As it is written in Isiah 10:27, *"It shall come to pass that this burden will be taken off of your shoulders, and the yoke shall be removed from your neck. And the yoke shall be destroyed."* That verse is not only for the addict but for their family and friends. This can be conquered.

Keep reminding your loved one that they are getting better, even when they are crawling to get there. Watch comedy shows together, and laugh until your tummies hurt. It's great therapy for everyone!

You may find it difficult to understand the addiction, and that is to be expected. People had no problem understanding that I had severe back pain, and they knew I was on a lot of medications. But I never said I was addicted to the pills because it would have totally changed their perception of me. That stigma is something we have to start changing, and I've got some other suggestions too.

Chapter 11

Blazing a Path for Others to Follow

"Work for a cause, not for applause.
Live life to express, not to impress.
Don't strive to make your presence noticed,
Just make your absence felt."
~ Grace Liechtenstein

This Is Not the Time for Anonymity

I'm not sure how I mentally and physically survived this terrible addiction. And yet, while I write these words, thousands, maybe even millions, of people are in the struggle of their lives, or tragically have already died, because of an opioid addiction. On a biological level, we are one and the same. I am no different, other than being successful in getting off those drugs. And if I've learned anything, it's this: I just can't sit idly by and DO NOTHING while others are struggling. I can't waste the life experience I've gained, or the new lease on life I've been gifted. While others' voices have been silenced by their death from opioids, I feel it's time for my voice to be heard.

I survived for a reason, and maybe it's to try to end the stigma of this terrible opioid epidemic. I didn't have aspirations to be known as someone who was an "opioid addict"; no one does. There isn't a career day on the planet that includes a booth staffed by addicts waiting to talk to those new recruits, who are aspiring to become addicted to OxyContin and other opioids.

The first stigma we need to tackle is self-blame. For me, personally, I relied on professional medical personnel to prescribe pain relief. I have great respect for doctors, nurses, nurse practitioners, and all medical personnel. The schooling that is required to become a doctor, nurse, or nurse practitioner, to name but a few, is tough. On top of that, you have residency, placements, and school loans that will haunt many for years. You take courses that I can't even begin to comprehend. I didn't go to school for years to do what you do; you are the experts. But as in any profession, you have the great, the good, and the awful. And when you are a compliant patient, the awful doctor can really harm you. And you let them because you TRUST them. But at the end of it all, none of this was MY FAULT. I didn't try to get high or try to chase a "fix"; I was just trying to get my pain under control. We have to stop blaming ourselves. It solves nothing and hinders us from moving forward.

Now, when I say the word "drug addict," your brain immediately goes to work finding a stored definition, and provides you with an image to help you understand the meaning. What image appears in your mind's eye? I bet it's not a pretty one, and it can even be quite frightening. If you are being honest, it certainly wouldn't be anyone you would voluntarily socialize with, would it? See, this is the next stigma that we, as a society, have to tackle. Some have suggested we change the term "drug addict," to "a person with a substance use disorder." I actually like that term better because it has no negativity attached.

I am putting my face and my voice out there to help end this stigma. I no longer take narcotics, as luckily, my pain is controlled by one pill a day now, a non-narcotic. I have no track marks on my arms, or any "evidence" on my body that I once was addicted to OxyContin. I am about as non-typical looking of a former addict as you could find. And THAT'S what I want people to see. We are like you. We are your neighbours, friends, and family members, and there are millions of us. Many still work daily and struggle with the effects of these drugs. We need to tackle this opioid crisis by acknowledging that the victims are everyday people who got trapped and need a way out. You cannot fix an opioid crisis if you are discriminating against those who are affected. It just won't happen.

Educate, Educate, Educate

The drug abuse not only affects the patient, but it also affects their family, their friends, the economy, and our communities as a whole. The opioid epidemic and the COVID pandemic are both killing people needlessly. The only difference is that there is no vaccine available for *this* drug epidemic. Opioids, when properly and ethically prescribed, are very effective at pain relief; however, in the wrong hands and overprescribed, they are chemically addictive and are dangerous to the health of all.

Initially, when OxyContin was introduced as the next best thing in pain control, doctors were deceived by Purdue Pharmacy. The true severity of addiction to this drug was hidden from our beloved professionals in order to sell more pills and make Purdue millions in profit. It was only after the addictions started to rise that lawsuits were filed, and Purdue admitted that it may have "skewed" the data to help sell OxyContin. But now that it is a known fact, we have to start spending more time educating doctors, nurses, patients, and future patients, with the real facts. Once you know better, you do better. There is a fine line between properly managing chronic pain with OxyContin or other medications, and overprescribing and causing addiction. Doctors need to have the proper drugs to control chronic pain. More training should be given to doctors and nurses, other than a half day that they currently receive on addiction.

But please understand, I'm not AGAINST narcotics at all. I am a strong advocate for doctors providing proper pain relief via opioids for those patients who are dealing with chronic pain.

That's what they were created to treat: severe pain. What I **AM** against are those doctors who are feeding this epidemic by improperly prescribing narcotics. Whether they are overprescribing them, just refilling prescriptions without proper follow-up, or are willing to make a quick buck, those are the doctors that need to be weeded out. Because of their lack of knowledge regarding the addictiveness of narcotics, lack of follow-up, or just sheer greed, their dangerous act of prescribing these narcotics has got to stop. We need to track those doctors who are prescribing massive amounts of narcotics needlessly, and revoke their licenses; and then throw them in jail and throw away the key. Or better yet, make them clean up rehabilitation bathrooms, because they were the ones that caused all of that mess!

Telling kids to "just say no," a program that was started back in the 1970s, doesn't seem to be as effective today. These young people are so much smarter now as the decades have ticked by. With drug use being much more prevalent and talked about, we need to give them better information about the dangers and addictive nature of these drugs. It isn't going to make them want to use them less, but it may save their lives. These drugs are everywhere and so easy to get; all you need to do is open a medicine cabinet in your home, in some cases. So, we can't put our heads in the sand and pretend that they don't know about them. They probably know more than you do. If their friends offer them a pill after school one day, having some real facts will help them make better decisions.

We also need to get away from the thought that you can only get off of these drugs if you go to a rehab centre. I don't understand why a doctor, who can throw all these exorbitant amounts of opioids at their patients, can't be trained to properly wean their patients off of these drugs. My pain specialist at the pain clinic lacked that ability, and that is TRULY shocking; she was a pain specialist!!!! Is it really that difficult? Are you addicted to OxyContin that you are getting legally from a doctor? Well, let's get that same doctor, or even another one, to wean you off of these drugs, slowly and safely, so that you can get your life back. Let's help addicts keep their jobs, their homes, and their children while becoming drug-free.

OxyContin was notoriously easy to crush, which destroyed the time release coating, allowing addicts to get the entire dosage all at once. So OxyNeo was introduced as the non-crushable, non-injectable OxyContin, to curb this behaviour, and illegal drug use on the streets decreased. That was an easy fix, or so they thought. Oh, but how resourceful bad people can be! It didn't take long for the illegal suppliers from China and South America to create a new "what looks like OxyContin" pill. Except it's NOT OxyContin; it's something even worse: fentanyl, or its even deadlier relative, carfentanyl—and this is causing even more overdoses and deaths. I truly don't know how you curb illegal drugs coming into our country, other than increasing the border security staff to hopefully catch more of the shipments. But these bad boys can be very resourceful in getting their drugs to their customers, and some of that involves bribes and the like.

Building a Support System

After all these years, when I see addicts on TV shows about addiction, I say to myself, *but for the Grace of God go I*. **That could have been me**—homeless, begging for any money to get the drugs, becoming a pro at criminal activities to get my drugs, being dope sick, and maybe even ending up dead. If I hadn't been able to get off the OxyContin, if I didn't have the love and support of my sister, Eley, my family, and my friends, and if I hadn't had the financial means to fund the withdrawal process, it would have been me. That's why we need to build a better support system.

I know I've said it before, but it bears repeating. If I didn't have my family and friends to help me during those 6 years of hell, up to the current day, I would not be alive today, period. They were there when I needed them, through all of it, and I am so blessed that they were. I don't believe I would have been successful without their guidance and love. I really mean that. So I truly believe that we need to build a better support system for addicts, because unfortunately, many of them don't have one.

Firstly, we need to have some standardization of care, and have an agency that will monitor these rehabilitation centres for compliance. Owners of addiction rehabilitation centres can make a lot of money without providing proper care and treatment. Again, it comes down to the great, the good, and the darn right ugly. When you are looking to get your loved one into a treatment centre, NOW, who has time to dig through mounds of brochures and information to find the most reputable one? Anyone can make a brochure look fabulous. And many of the best ones are booked solid, so when you find an open bed, you are ecstatic to finally get in. But there can be a real shock when the addict shows up at the "center," only to find they had better living conditions in the rooming house they just left. We need to be sifting through these places, and closing down the appalling places that are a disgrace to those centers who are helping addicts.

Secondly, we need to establish a hotline or toll-free number for those going through withdrawal. Many addicts may not feel comfortable calling a friend or family member, but would call someone who doesn't care what their name is and doesn't know them. Those providing guidance at those hotlines would have the proper training to initiate any additional care or advice that is required. Not everyone has a sponsor on call 24/7 to help them.

Thirdly, for those who have to find illegal drugs because the legally prescribed drugs are too expensive, there has got to be a way to help them out financially while they are withdrawing. The doctor prescribed them these amounts to get them hooked, so there has got to be a way to provide them with the same drug, at either a lower cost option or free, if they really can't afford it. The addict would have to prove that they are continuing to follow the withdrawal process with their doctor. It would be a win-win for society and the addict. It would decrease illegal drug activity and all of the costs (security, hospital visits, reduced theft) associated with it, and the addict would eventually be drug free.

We need to introduce better policies to help those who are addicted. Instead of throwing addicts into a prison, why don't we address the real reason for them getting illegal drugs: they are sick. Now, I'm thinking of a perfect world here, but why can't we put them into a rehabilitation program instead of putting them in jail. Their sickness is the real issue, and putting them in our already crowded jails doesn't help anyone. You are risking the addict's life if they are having to withdraw in jail, as going "cold turkey" could kill them. And where can you get a crash course on how to do more illegal things? JAIL. We need to realize that we are just treating a symptom of the real issue, and if we continue, it won't solve anything.

I believe that we need to have more guidance and services available for those going through withdrawal while remaining at home, which includes the caregiver and roommates. There needs to be information for all, on what to expect, where to get extra help for caregiver respite care, and any other questions they may have. We were lucky to have such great doctors to oversee the withdrawal plan, but knowing what to expect would have been helpful. Eley certainly could have benefitted from some time away from me, so that she could recharge her batteries. Anything would have been helpful.

There Is Hope!

I want to give you hope that you, too, can get free of these drugs. I am no different than you are. I, too, am a human being that got off OxyContin without going into a drug addiction centre or program. I did not go through a "medically supervised detox" either. I removed these drugs from my system over many months, with the help of my family doctor and my specialist (because of my back injury). At times, you will feel like you are going

50 steps backwards, but keep taking it one day at a time. You are strong, and you are capable. **YOU CAN BE DRUG FREE TOO!!** I won't give you a false promise that it's easy, because it isn't. It is really, really difficult. But the life waiting for you at the end of this will be so worth the struggle. And if I can help just ONE person by telling my story, then my soul will be happy. I hope you are that one.